Dictionary of Islamic Names

Derived from Qur'ān, Ahādîth, Seerah and History

First Edition: January 2008

Supervised by:

Abdul Malik Mujahid

HEAD OFFICE

P.O. Box: 22743, Riyadh 11416 K.S.A.Tel: 00966-1-4033962/4043432 Fax: 4021659
E-mail: darussalam@awalnet.net.sa, riyadh@dar-us-salam.com Website: www.dar-us-salam.com

K.S.A. Darussalam Showrooms:

Riyadh

Olaya branch: Tel 00966-1-4614483 Fax: 4644945
Malaz branch: Tel 00966-1-4735220 Fax: 4735221
Suwailam branch: Tel & Fax-1-2860422

- **Jeddah**
  Tel: 00966-2-6879254 Fax: 6336270
- **Madinah**
  Tel: 00966-04-8234446, 8230038
  Fax: 04-8151121
- **Al-Khobar**
  Tel: 00966-3-8692900 Fax: 8691551
- **Khamis Mushayt**
  Tel & Fax: 00966-072207055
- **Yanbu Al-Bahr** Tel: 0500887341 Fax: 04-3908027
- **Al-Buraida** Tel: 0503417156 Fax: 06-3696124

U.A.E
- **Darussalam, Sharjah U.A.E**
  Tel: 00971-6-5632623 Fax: 5632624
  Sharjah@dar-us-salam.com.

PAKISTAN
- **Darussalam,** 36 B Lower Mall, Lahore
  Tel: 0092-42-724 0024 Fax: 7354072
- **Rahman Market, Ghazni Street,** Urdu Bazar Lahore
  Tel: 0092-42-7120054 Fax: 7320703
- **Karachi,** Tel: 0092-21-4393936 Fax: 4393937
- **Islamabad,** Tel: 0092-51-2500237 Fax: 512281513

U.S.A
- **Darussalam, Houston**
  P.O Box: 79194 Tx 77279
  Tel: 001-713-722 0419 Fax: 001-713-722 0431
  E-mail: houston @dar-us-salam.com
- **Darussalam, New York** 486 Atlantic Ave, Brooklyn
  New York-11217, Tel: 001-718-625 5925
  Fax: 718-625 1511
  E-mail: darussalamny@hotmail.com

U.K
- **Darussalam International Publications Ltd.**
  Leyton Business Centre
  Unit-17, Etloe Road, Leyton, London, E10 7BT
  Tel: 0044 20 8539 4885 Fax:0044 20 8539 4889
  Website: www.darussalam.com
  Email: info@darussalam.com
- **Darussalam International Publications Limited**
  Regents Park Mosque, 146 Park Road
  London NW8 7RG Tel: 0044- 207 725 2246
  Fax: 0044 20 8539 4889

AUSTRALIA
- **Darussalam:** 153, Haldon St, Lakemba (Sydney)
  NSW 2195, Australia
  Tel: 0061-2-97407188 Fax: 0061-2-97407199
  Mobile: 0061-414580813 Res: 0061-2-97580190
  Email: abumuaaz@hotamail.com

CANADA
- **Nasser Khattab**
  2-3415 Dixie Rd, Unit # 505
  Mississauga
  Ontario L4Y 4J6, Canada
  Tel: 001-416-418 6619
- **Islamic Book Service**
  2200 South Sheridan way Mississauga, On
  L5J 2M4
  Tel: 001-905-403-8406 Ext. 218 Fax: 905-8409

MALAYSIA
- **Darussalam**
  Int'l Publishing & Distribution SDN BHD
  D-2-12, Setiawangsa 11, Taman Setiawangsa
  54200 Kuala Lumpur
  Tel: 03-42528200 Fax: 03-42529200
  Email: darussalam@streamyx.com
  Website: www.darussalam.com.my

FRANCE
- **Editions & Librairie Essalam**
  135, Bd de Ménilmontant- 75011 Paris
  Tél: 0033-01- 43 38 19 56/ 44 83
  Fax: 0033-01- 43 57 44 31
  E-mail: essalam@essalam com.

SINGAPORE
- **Muslim Converts Association of Singapore**
  32 Onan Road The Galaxy
  Singapore- 424484
  Tel: 0065-440 6924, 348 8344 Fax: 440 6724

SRI LANKA
- Darul Kitab 6, Nimal Road, Colombo-4
  Tel: 0094 115 358712 Fax: 115-358713

INDIA
- **Islamic Books International**
  54, Tandel Street (North)
  Dongri, Mumbai 4000 09, INDIA
  Tel: 0091-22-2373 4180
  E-mail: ibi@irf.net

SOUTH AFRICA
- **Islamic Da'wah Movement (IDM)**
  48009 Qualbert 4078 Durban,South Africa
  Tel: 0027-31-304-6883 Fax: 0027-31-305-1292
  E-mail: idm@ion.co.za

Dictionary of Islamic Names

Derived from Qur'ān, Ahādîth, Seerah and History
With Meaning and Pronunciation

Compiled by:
Prof. Hafiz Shaukat Ali Hareeri and
Hafiz Muhammad Ikram Tahir

DARUSSALAM

بسم الله الرحمن الرحيم

In the Name of Allāh, the Most Gracious, the Most Merciful

King Fahd National Library Cataloging-in-Publication Data
Hareeri, Hafiz Shaukat Ali
Dictionary of Islamic names derived from Quraan, Ahadith, Serah and history with meaning and pronunciatin. / Hafiz Shaukat Ali Hareeri - Riyadh, 2009
238p ; 14x21 cm

ISBN: 978-603-500-029-1

1-Names, Personal - Islamic 2- Names Dictionaries 1-Title
929.4 dc 1430/5032
L.D. no. 1430/5032
ISBN: 978-603-500-029-1

Contents

Publisher's Note 11

Chapter:1

The Teachings and Injunctions about a Neonate Baby 17

The Role of Parents or Guardian at the Birth of a Baby 18

The Injunctions about Sharing the Joy and Felicitations on the Birth of a Baby 19

Proof of Congratulation from the Holy Qur'ān 20

- Historical Proof 21
- Proof of Congratulation 21

The Injunctions about Pronouncing the *Adhān* (Call for Prayer) in the Baby's Ear 23

- Implied Benefits of *Adhān*: 23
- The Teachings and Injunctions about *Tahnīk* (Baby's Initial Food) 25
- What is *Tahnīk?* 25
- Advantage of *Tahnīk* 25
- Who should Have the Honor of *Tahnīk* 25
- Proof of *Tahnīk* from *Hadīth* 25

- The Practice of Imām Ahmad bin Hanbal رحمۃ اللہ علیہ 27

Shaving off the Baby's Hair 28

- Advantages of Shaving off the Baby's Hair. 28
- Prophet's Sunnah about Shaving the Baby's Head 28
- The Custom of *Qazā*' 29
- Types of *Qazā*' 30
- Why *Qazā*' is Forbidden? 30

Chapter:2

The Rules and Principles about Giving Name and Surname to the Children 32

When should a Baby be Given a Name? 33

Desirable and the Undesirable Names 36

- The Best Names 36
- Undesirable and Evil Names 36
- Of the Undesirable and Evil Names 36
- Philosophy of Good and Bad Names 44
- A Comprehensive *Hadīth* about Names 44

The Rules and Principles for Giving *Kunyah* (Surname) 46

Importance of Giving a Surname to a Child according to the *Sharī'ah* 47

Practice of the Companions of the Prophet ﷺ 48

Miscellaneous Rules and Principles about Name, Title and Surname 50

- Bad Names and Titles 51
- For Parents and Guardians 53

Chapter:3

Allāh's Beautiful Names 54
Attributive Names of Allāh Almighty 55

Chapter:4

Names of the Messenger of Allaḥ ﷺ 70
The Noble Prophets عليهم السلام 73
Names of the Wives رضي الله عنهن of the Prophet ﷺ 76
Children of the Prophet ﷺ 78
The Ten Blessed Companions رضي الله عنهم who were Given the Glad Tiding of Paradise 79
The Martyrs of the Battle of Badr 80
The Participants of the Battle of Badr from the *Muhajirūn* (Emigrants) 81
The Participants of the Battle of Badr from the *Ansār* (Helpers) 87
The Commander Companions رضي الله عنهم of the Prophet ﷺ 102
The Eminent Female Companions رضي الله عنهن of the Messenger of Allah ﷺ 104
The Female Companions رضي الله عنهن Who Learned the Qur'ān by Heart 106
The Female Companions رضي الله عنهن Who Learned a Portion of the Qur'ān 106
The Exegete amongst the Female Companions رضي الله عنهن 106
The Traditionists amongst the Female Companions رضي الله عنهن of the Prophet ﷺ 107
The Jurist and Scholar Female Companions رضي الله عنهن 107

The Expert in Heritage amongst the Female Companions رضي الله عنهما 108

The Expert Female Companion رضي الله عنهما in the Secrets of Sharī'aḥ 108

The Orator Female Companion رضي الله عنهما 109

The Interpreter of Dreams 109

The Expert Female Companions رضي الله عنهن in the Science of Medicine and Surgery 109

The Eminent Poetess amongst the Female Companions رضي الله عنهن 110

The Scribes amongst the Female Companions رضي الله عنهن of the Prophet ﷺ 111

The Traders amongst the Female Companions رضي الله عنهن of the Prophet ﷺ 111

Chapter:5

Qur'ānic Names for the Muslim Males 113

Qur'ānic Names for the Muslim Females 139

Chapter:6

Islamic Names for the Muslim Males 157

Islamic Names for the Muslim Females 200

Publisher's Note

The first lesson given to Adam عليه السلام after his creation was the knowledge of names, which established his superiority over the angels, and became the reason for their prostration to him. Although the Holy Qur'ān does not give the names that Adam عليه السلام was taught, it does say that the earliest form of knowledge imparted to man by his Creator was the knowledge of names. The first lesson also established the identity of objects and human beings from the beginning. Through the Holy Qur'ān the Creator got Himself identified by His Name (Allāh) and reinforced this identity through His various Attributive Names, asserting that one can call Him by anyone of His beautiful names, as the Holy Qur'ān says:

﴿وَلِلَّهِ الْأَسْمَاءُ الْحُسْنَىٰ﴾

"The Most Beautiful Names belong to Allāh."

Besides the identity of the individual, names also reflect the religion, moral values, nation and the country of persons. Therefore, neonate babies should be given good names. Children are a great blessing of Allāh, termed as blossoms of Paradise by the Messenger of Allāh ﷺ. The best way of expressing joy on the birth of a child is to express gratitude to Allāh for this favor. Feeling hurt and disappointed at the birth of a daughter is against the teachings of Islām, and unbecoming for a Muslim. In the Holy Qur'ān Allāh asserts that:

> "To Allāh belongs the kingdom of the heavens and the earth. He creates what He wills. He bestows female (offspring) upon whom He wills, and bestows male (offspring) upon whom He wills, Or He bestows both males and females, and He renders barren whom He wills."[1]

Therefore, daughters too should be regarded as a blessing, not as a curse. The Prophet ﷺ has repeatedly assured entry to Paradise of those who treat their daughters with love and care.

In a Muslim family it is necessary to clean the newly born baby and make him hear the Holy Names of Allāh and the Prophet ﷺ by reciting the *'Adhān* (call for prayer) in his right ear, and *'Iqāmah* (the final call for prayer) in his left ear. It is also good to place the baby on the lap of a pious elderly person for being blessed by that person as 'Asmā had put her baby 'Abdullāh ؓ on the lap of Prophet Muhammad ﷺ. Also the baby should be made to taste something already tasted by some pious person. Usually dates, or something sweet of similar kind is chewed by a pious person and applied to the baby's palate. Then the pious person should pray for the baby to be blessed.

On the seventh day of the baby's birth, the head should be shaved, alms to be given away, the ritual of *'Aqīqah* to be performed and a beautiful name should be given to the baby.

[1] [Ash-Shūrā: 42:49,50]

The baby's head must be shaved on the 7th day, and silver

equal in weight to the baby's shaved off hair or money amounting to the price of silver, should be given away as alms.

The Prophet ﷺ laid special stress on the performance of *'Aqīqah* saying that every child is a pawn against *'Aqīqah*, therefore, this ritual should by performed on the seventh day. The Prophet ﷺ said:

> "Two animals should be slaughtered as *'Aqīqah* for the male baby, and one for the female."

If the parents cannot afford *'Aqīqah* on the seventh day, they may perform the ritual whenever it is possible.

Giving name to the baby on the seventh day is also desirable and in accordance with the practice of the Prophet ﷺ. However, the baby may as well be named earlier, as the name may be decided even before its birth. Circumcising the male baby on the seventh day is also better than later.

Naming the baby is also an expression of gratitude to Allāh for this blessing. Names not only give the child an identity, but also deeply influence his or her personality. It is, therefore, the duty of the parents to give the baby a meaningful, beautiful and Islāmic name. The Prophet ﷺ has directed the Muslims to give their babies good names and refrain from such names which carry evil sense or claim parity (*Shirk*) with Allāh. There are many examples to prove that the Prophetﷺ replaced bad names with good ones so that the ill-named person might not develop the bad attributes implied by his or her name. For instance, in one case he replaced the name حَزْن [Hazn] "Hard ground" with سَهْل [Sahl] "Soft or easy".

Inferring good omen from a good name is exactly in

accordance with the practice of the Prophet ﷺ. For instance, on the occasion of the peace treaty signed at Hudaibiyyah, when a man, named Suhail, came to represent the Quraish of Makkah, the Prophet ﷺ said that his good name would pave the way to the peace process. As a name deeply influences the personality, the Prophet ﷺ advised his followers to name their babies carefully. He said:

"The names most pleasing to Allāh are عَبْدُالله ['Abdullāh] and عبدُالرحمن ['Abdur Rahmān], حَارِث [Hārith] and همَّام [Hammām] are the most truthful names, and حَرْب [Harb] "War" and مُرَّة [Murrah] "Bitter" are the worst of names."

The names of Prophets عليهم السلام are best next to the names of Allāh. Attributive names of Prophet Muhammad ﷺ are the most eminent and blessed ones. So the Prophet ﷺ asked his followers to name their children after him. The babies may be named after the various attributive names of the Prophet ﷺ given in the Holy Qur'ān and books of *Hadīth*. All Prophets and Messengers عليهم السلام are honorable and loved by Allāh, so babies may also be named after them. The Prophet ﷺ said:

"Name your babies after the Prophets."

Naming a baby after them shows affiliation with those illustrious figures, and keeps their memories alive.

Making a bad nickname is not a desirable practice, although it is quite common in the society. Those who indulge in this practice, don't realize that it is an insult to spoil the sanctified names of Allāh, the Prophet ﷺ and pious figures of Islāmic history. It is a sin and it may incur the wrath of Allāh. There is, however, no harm in shortening a name to express love for the child or person, provided that it is not a degradation of an Islāmic name. For instance, the Prophet ﷺ sometimes addressed Abū Hurairah ؓ with "Abū Hur ؓ" and his own wife 'Ā'ishah ؓ with 'Ā'ish. Hence shortening a name is lawful.

The best names are those which are meaningful, Islāmic and pleasant to hear. The importance of giving beautiful names to the children can be estimated from the fact that the Islāmic *Sharī'ah* prescribes special norms for naming the Muslim children. It has also enjoined on the parents to look after every need of the children from feeding the baby to his proper education and marriage when he grows up to the marriageable age. It also makes compulsory that all children should be treated with equal love and affection. Each of them should be given his due share in inheritance. The parents are advised to pray for the welfare of their children, and bear the loss of a son or daughter by death with patience, praying for his or her forgiveness.

Although several books on this subject are available in the market but this book is different for the following qualities.

- The beautiful Names of Allāh, the Almighty, and the Prophet ﷺ are given along with one reference at least to make them more interesting and useful. However, we have been very brief and to the point.
- Names of the Prophet's Companions ؓ are also given in a large number, although some of them are not so meaningful yet they may be adopted to express affiliation with the pious figures.
- Quality of the names has been preferred to the quantity

against the norm of the books of names.

- Only selected names of beautiful meaning and sound have been given.

Indicator of vowel sounds have been used to ensure the correct pronunciation of the names.

A few undesirable names are also given so that the people may avoid such names.

The Islāmic injunctions and teachings about the birth of a baby have been taken from the book *"Ahkam-ul-Mawlud-ul-Muslim"* By Jamāl Zaki Hawarī رحمه الله. This book is a truly distinct achievement among the books on this subject.

I conclude this introduction with the prayer that may Allāh bless us with the spirit to take care of the new generation and give them truly Islāmic, meaningful and beautiful names.

Abdul Malik Mujahid
General Manager
Darussalam

Chapter:1

The Teachings and Injunctions about a Neonate Baby

- Congratulating on the Birth of a Baby
- Calling *Adhān* (Call for Prayer) in the Baby's Ear
- Details of *Tahnīk*, Shaving off the Head and its Implied Benefits.

The Role of Parents or Guardian at the Birth of a Baby

Thanks to the Islāmic Sharī'ah which has laid down all the necessary injunctions and rules to be observed at the birth of a Muslim baby, and has stated in detail all the factors that influence the upbringing of children. A person knowing these details can very well cope with the duties and obligations related to proper upbringing of a baby.

Everyone, who is entrusted with a baby to look after, should handle this responsibility in accordance with the rules laid down by Islām, following the advice and practice of the Prophet ﷺ in letter and spirit. Now we shall give the details of these basic rules and practices:

The Injunctions about Sharing the Joy and Felicitations on the Birth of a Baby

If the father is not present, then the relatives who know about the birth, should inform him about the baby's birth, and congratulate him. They should also pray for the health and well being of the baby.

It is obligatory for a Muslim to share the happy news with others. Therefore, if someone is blessed with a baby, he should at once convey the news to his dear ones, because it would be beneficial in the following ways:

- It promotes goodwill and strengthens relations among relatives
- It establishes cordial and sincere friendship
- It promotes social contacts
- It promotes feeling of brotherhood and strengthens the Islāmic society

If the news of the baby's birth is not received immediately, even then it is a moral duty of friends and relatives of the family to acknowledge the information whenever it comes by congratulating the parents and praying for the family.

Proof of Congratulation from the Holy Qur'ān

The Holy Qur'ān has repeatedly highlighted the importance of congratulation on the birth of a child as it will enhance fraternity and brotherhood and will be beneficial for the Muslim community. The Holy Qur'ān tells us the story of Ibrāhīm (Abraham) عليه السلام and his reaction to the angels:

﴿وَلَقَدْ جَآءَتْ رُسُلُنَآ إِبْرَٰهِيمَ بِٱلْبُشْرَىٰ قَالُوا۟ سَلَٰمًا ۖ قَالَ سَلَٰمٌ ۖ فَمَا لَبِثَ أَن جَآءَ
بِعِجْلٍ حَنِيذٍ ﴿٦٩﴾ فَلَمَّا رَءَآ أَيْدِيَهُمْ لَا تَصِلُ إِلَيْهِ نَكِرَهُمْ وَأَوْجَسَ مِنْهُمْ
خِيفَةً ۚ قَالُوا۟ لَا تَخَفْ إِنَّآ أُرْسِلْنَآ إِلَىٰ قَوْمِ لُوطٍ ﴿٧٠﴾ وَٱمْرَأَتُهُۥ قَآئِمَةٌ فَضَحِكَتْ
فَبَشَّرْنَٰهَا بِإِسْحَٰقَ وَمِن وَرَآءِ إِسْحَٰقَ يَعْقُوبَ ﴿٧١﴾﴾

"And verily, there came our messengers to Ibrāhīm (Abraham) with glad tidings. They said: *Salām* (greeting or peace!). He answered: *Salām* (greeting or peace!) and he hastened to entertain them with a roasted calf. But when he saw their hands went not towards it (the meal), he mistrusted them, and conceived a fear of them. They said: "Fear not, we have been sent against the people of Lūt (Lot). And his wife was standing (there), and she laughed [either, because the messengers did not eat their food or for being glad for the destruction of the people of

Lūt (Lot)]. But We gave her glad tidings of Ishāq (Isaac). And after Ishāq, of Ya'qūb (Jacob)."[1]

Allāh The Almighty says about Zakariyyā (Zachariya) عليه السلام:

﴿فَنَادَتْهُ ٱلْمَلَٰٓئِكَةُ وَهُوَ قَآئِمٌ يُصَلِّى فِى ٱلْمِحْرَابِ أَنَّ ٱللَّهَ يُبَشِّرُكَ بِيَحْيَىٰ﴾

"Then the angels called him, while he was standing in prayer in Al-Mihrāb (a praying place or a private room), (saying) "Allāh gives you glad tidings of Yahyā (John)."[2]

The story of glad tidings to Zakariyyā (Zachariya) عليه السلام is repeated in the words:

﴿يَٰزَكَرِيَّآ إِنَّا نُبَشِّرُكَ بِغُلَٰمٍ ٱسْمُهُۥ يَحْيَىٰ لَمْ نَجْعَل لَّهُۥ مِن قَبْلُ سَمِيًّا﴾

"(Allāh said) O Zakariyyā (Zachariah)! Verily, We give you the glad tidings of a son, whose name will be Yahyā (John). We have given that name to none before (him)."[3]

Historical Proof:

Imām Ibn Qayyim رحمه الله says:

"When the Prophet ﷺ was born, Thuwaiba, the female slave of the Prophet's uncle Abū Lahab, conveyed the good news to Abū Lahab, saying "Allāh has granted your brother Abdullāh, a son. Abū Lahab was overjoyed and he freed the lady."[4]

Proof of Congratulation:

Imām Ibn Qayyim رحمه الله, in his book "*Tuhfat-ul-Maudūd*" reports from Abū Bakr bin Mundhir that once a man was sitting with Hasan Basarī رحمه الله. Another man came and congratulated

[1] [Hūd 11:69,70] [2] [Āl-'Imrān: 3:39]

[3] [Maryam 19:7] [4] [Bukhārī: 5101]

him saying: "Congratulation on the birth of a horseman." Hasan Basarī رحمة الله عليه said, "How do you know whether neonate baby will be a horseman or a donkey rider?" He asked them then how we could congratulate anybody?" He said: "The birth of a baby should be felicitated by saying: "May Allāh bless the gift (of a baby) with long life and enable him to treat you well. And you should also be thankful to Allāh Who has blessed you with this gift."[1]

Warning: Birth of a female as well as a male baby should be equally regarded as a blessing. There should be no dis-discrimination on the basis of sex or race.

It is the duty of all the Muslims to follow the example of the Prophet ﷺ and make it a social norm to ensure goodwill and brotherhood among the Muslims. In this way the Muslims could be united and make a strong force capable of facing every challenge. It is mandatory for all of the Muslims to develop harmony and brotherhood and they should be as united as the bricks in a wall where every brick strengthens the other.

[1] [Tuhfat-ul-Maudūd: 52]

The Injunctions about Pronouncing the *Adhān* (Call for Prayer) in the Baby's Ear

One of the measures pertaining to the birth of a baby according to the *Islāmic Shari'ah* is pronouncing the *Adhān* in his/ her ear.

Abū Rāfi' ﷺ reports that:

«رَأَيْتُ رَسُولَ اللهِ ﷺ أَذَّنَ فِي أُذُنِ الْحَسَنِ بْنِ عَلِيٍّ، حِينَ وَلَدَتْهُ فَاطِمَةُ، بِالصَّلَاةِ»

"When Hasan bin 'Alī, son of the Prophet's daughter Fātimah ﷺ, was born, I saw the Prophet ﷺ pronouncing the *Adhān* (call for prayer) in his ear."[1]

Implied benefits of *Adhān*:

Some of the important benefits of the *Adhān* are briefly given below:

1. The first benefit is that the baby, first of all hears the words which express the supremacy of Allāh. The pronouncement of the *Adhān* is also a reminder of the faith which was enjoined

[1] [Abū Dawūd: 5105,Tuhfat-ul-Maudūd: 53]

on man at the time of his creation. Similarly when he is leaving the world, his faith is reinforced by advising him to recite the *Kalima Tayyebah*, as the Prophet ﷺ says:

«لَقِّنُوا مَوْتَاكُمْ لَا إِلٰهَ إِلَّا اللهُ»

"Advise your dying people to recite "*Lā-Ilāha Illallāh*" [1]

2. Of course Allāh can affect the baby's heart with words recited in his/her ears, although those around the child cannot see how it happens.

3. The words of the *Adhān* drive away Satan who is always around to mislead a newly born baby.[2]

The words of the *Adhān* pronounced in the baby's ear would protect the baby from the influence of Satan, and he will go back writhing in frustration.

4. The world is a place of trial and therefore, the newly born Muslim baby is fortified against Satan with holy words of faith in the form of the *Adhān*. Every child is born with the natural faith of Islām but Satan does his best to mislead him from the natural track of true faith, and turn him into an unbeliever.

5. The advantages of the *Adhān* recounted by Imām Ibn Qayyim رحمه الله makes it clear that all of the Muslim scholars gave special importance to teaching the basics of faith. So much so that soon after the birth of a baby true Islāmic faith is pronounced to him in order to protect him against Satan's temptation to evil ways.

[1] [Muslim: 916, Abū Dawūd: 3117]

[2] [Bukhārī: 5823]

The Teachings and Injunctions about *Tahnīk* (Baby's Initial Food):

It is believed that if the baby shares the food chewed by a pious person, it is hoped that the baby will also share the moral qualities of that person. The practice of *Tahnīk* is confirmed by the reported *Sunnah* of the Prophet ﷺ and practice of the other pious figures in Islāmic history.

What is *Tahnīk*?

The food, preferably dates, fruit or any other sweet eatable, in accordance with the performance of the Prophet ﷺ, is chewed and then a bit of it is gently applied to the baby's palate. Grape or sweetened curd mixed with rose water was also used by the Prophet ﷺ.

Advantage of *Tahnīk*:

It is believed that as the baby rubs its tongue against the palate to swallow the initial food, its mouth and tongue muscles start functioning to suck the mother's milk more easily.

Who should have the honor of *Tahnīk*?

Tahnīk should be done by a person of known piety so that the moral and spiritual qualities of such a person may be transmitted to the baby.

Proof of *Tahnīk* from *Hadīth*:

The practice of *Tahnīk* is reported in the sayings of the Holy Prophet ﷺ. The scholars of *Fiqh* referred to the following *Ahādīth* in the context of this practice. Abū Mūsā Ash'arī رضي الله عنه narrated:

«وُلِدَ لِي غُلَامٌ، فَأَتَيْتُ بِهِ النَّبِيَّ ﷺ فَسَمَّاهُ إِبْرَاهِيمَ، فَحَنَّكَهُ

بِتَمْرَةٍ وَدَعَا لَهُ بِالْبَرَكَةِ وَدَفَعَهُ إِلَيَّ»

"A son was born to me and I took him to the Prophet ﷺ who named him Ibrāhīm, did *Tahnīk* for him with a date, invoked Allāh to bless him and returned him to me."[1]

Anas ﷺ narrated:

«كَانَ ابْنٌ لِأَبِي طَلْحَةَ يَشْتَكِي فَخَرَجَ أَبُوطَلْحَةَ فَقُبِضَ الصَّبِيُّ، فَلَمَّا رَجَعَ أَبُوطَلْحَةَ، قَالَ: مَا فَعَلَ ابْنِي؟ قَالَتْ أُمُّ سُلَيمٍ: هُوَ أَسْكَنُ مَا كَانَ، فَقَرَّبَتْ إِلَيْهِ الْعَشَاءَ فَتَعَشَّى ثُمَّ أَصَابَ مِنْهَا، فَلَمَّا فَرَغَ قَالَتْ: وَارُوا الصَّبِيَّ، فَلَمَّا أَصْبَحَ أَبُوطَلْحَةَ أَتَى رَسُولَ اللهِ ﷺ فَأَخْبَرَهُ فَقَالَ: أَعَرَسْتُمُ اللَّيْلَةَ؟ قَالَ: نَعَمْ! قَالَ: اللَّهُمَّ! بَارِكْ لَهُمَا فَوَلَدَتْ غُلَامًا، فَقَالَ لِي أَبُوطَلْحَةَ: إِحْمِلْهُ حَتَّى تَأْتِيَ بِهِ النَّبِيَّ ﷺ فَأَتَى بِهِ النَّبِيَّ ﷺ وَبَعَثَتْ مَعَهُ بِتَمَرَاتٍ، فَأَخَذَهُ النَّبِيُّ ﷺ فَقَالَ: أَمَعَهُ شَيْءٌ؟ قَالُوا: نَعَمْ، تَمَرَاتٌ، فَأَخَذَهَا النَّبِيُّ ﷺ فَمَضَغَهَا، ثُمَّ أَخَذَهَا مِنْ فِيهِ، فَجَعَلَهَا فِي فِي الصَّبِيِّ، ثُمَّ حَنَّكَهُ، وَسَمَّاهُ عَبْدَاللهِ»

Abū Talhah had a child who was sick. The child died when Abū Talhah had gone out. When Abū Talhah ﷺ returned home, he asked, "How does my son fare?" Umm Sulaim (his wife) replied, "He is quieter than he has ever been." Then she brought for him and he took his supper and slept with her. When he had finished, she said (to him),

[1] [Bukhārī: 5467, Muslim:2145]

"Bury the child (as he's dead)." Next morning Abū Talhah came to Allāh's Messenger ﷺ and told him about that. The Prophet ﷺ said (to him), "Did you sleep with your wife last night?" Abū Talhah said, "Yes". The Prophet ﷺ said, "O Allāh! Bestow your blessing on them as regards that night of theirs." Then (later on) Umm Sulaim gave birth to a boy. Abū Talhah told me (Anas رضي الله عنه) to take care of the child till he was taken to the Prophet ﷺ. Abū Talhah took the child to the Prophet ﷺ and Umm Sulaim sent some dates along with the child. The Prophet ﷺ took the child (on his lap) and asked if there was something with him. He replied, "Yes, a few dates". The Prophet ﷺ took a date, chewed it, took some of it out of his mouth, put it into the child's mouth and did *Tahnīk* for him with that and named him Abdullāh."[1]

The Practice of Imām Ahmad bin Hanbal رحمه الله

Khallāl رحمه الله reports from Muhammad bin 'Alī رحمه الله about the female slave who gave birth to Ahamd's son "Sa'īd". She said that when she gave birth to Sa'īd Imām Ahmad called for a date, brought from Makkah, and he asked, Umm 'Alī to chew and apply it to the baby's palate.[2]

[1] [Bukhārī : 5470, Muslim : 2144.]

[2] [Tuhfat-ul-Moudūd: 56]

Shaving off the Baby's Hair

It is an established edict of Prophet Muhammad ﷺ that on the seventh day of a baby's birth, the head should be shaved and silver, equivalent to the weight of the shaved off hair, should be given away as alms to the poor and the needy.

Advantages of shaving off the baby's hair.

There are two advantages of this practice:

1. Beneficial for health: Exposure of the baby's head to fresh open air, and easy massaging of the head improves the baby's health, especially the five senses.

2. Promotion of charitable acts: Giving away silver or equivalent money to the poor promotes the passion of charity and helps in improving the economy of the poor in an Islāmic society. Helping the poor and supporting the needy is an act, generally eulogized in Islām. And by such acts of charity fraternity and brotherhood develop among all members of the community.

The Prophet's *Sunnah* about Shaving the Baby's Head:

Muhammad Bāqir bin 'Alī رحمه الله narrated:

«وَزَنَتْ فَاطِمَةُ بِنْتُ رَسُولِ اللهِ ﷺ شَعْرَ حَسَنٍ وَحُسَيْنٍ وَزَيْنَبَ

وَأُمِّ كُلْثُومٍ فَتَصَدَّقَتْ بِزِنَةِ ذٰلِكَ فِضَّةً»

"Fātimah, the daughter of the Prophet ﷺ got the shaved hair of her sons, Hasan and Hussain, and daughters Zainab and Umm Kulthūm ﵃, she weighed and gave away the equivalent weight of silver to the poor."[1]

'Alī ﵁ narrates:

«عَقَّ رَسُولُ اللهِ ﷺ عَنِ الْحَسَنِ بِشَاةٍ وَقَالَ: يَافَاطِمَةُ احْلِقِي رَأْسَهُ وَتَصَدَّقِي بِزِنَةِ شَعْرِهِ فِضَّةً»

"The Messenger of Allāh ﷺ slaughtered a goat and gave away its meat as 'Aqīqah of his grandson Hassan, and said to his daughter Fatimah ﵂, "Fātimah, get the baby's head shaved and, then give away equivalent weight of silver in charity."[2]

Anas bin Mālik ﵁ narrated:

«أَنَّ رَسُولَ اللهِ ﷺ أَمَرَ بِرَأْسِ الْحَسَنِ وَالْحُسَيْنِ ابْنَيْ عَلِيِّ بْنِ أَبِي طَالِبٍ يَوْمَ سَابِعِهِمَا، فَحُلِّقَ، ثم تَصَدَّقَ بِوَزْنِهِ فِضَّةً»

"The Messenger of Allāh ﷺ directed 'Alī ﵁ on the seventh day after the birth of Hasan and Hussain ﵄ to get their heads shaved and then he gave away silver of equivalent weight in charity."[3]

The Custom of *Qazā*':

Qazā' means, partial shaving of a baby's hair. It is a gross

[1] [Muwatta Imām Mālik: 1110]

[2] [Tirmidhī: 1519, Irwā': 175.]

[3] [Mu'jam al-'Awsat, Tabarānī: 1/50, Irwā': 4/405]

violation of the rules of the Islāmic *Shari'ah*. Abdullah bin Umar ﷺ narrated:

«أَنَّ رَسُولَ اللهِ ﷺ نَهَى عَنِ الْقَزَعِ»

"The Mesenger of Allāh ﷺ forbade Qazā'."[1]

Types of *Qazā'*:

There are four types of Qazā':

1. Shaving off the hair from various parts of the head
2. Shaving from the hair only in the center of head
3. Leaving only a tuft of hair in the center
4. Shaving off only the front half of the hair

Why *Qazā'* is forbidden?

'Allāmah Ibn Qayyim رحمه الله says that *Qazā'* is forbidden because Islām appreciates justice and balance whereas *Qazā'* is a form of injustice and imbalance. The Prophet ﷺ has forbidden sitting astride light and shade because it is an injustice to half of the body that is exposed to heat of the sun.[2] Similarly he has forbidden wearing one shoe as it is an injustice to the exposed foot. He said:

"Either wear both the shoes or go bare footed".[3]

The Prophet ﷺ wished the Muslims to put on a graceful appearance as much as they can afford. Partial shaving of the head gives an ugly look, therefore, it is unIslāmic.

Regrettably, most of the Muslim parents and guardians

[1] [Bukhārī: 5921, Muslim: 2120]

[2] [Ibn Mājah: 3722, Musnad Ahmad: 3/414]

[3] [Bukhārī: 5855, Muslim: 2097]

ignore such minor despoils and try to justify the violation of Islāmic rules. Having knowledge of such rules is very important for every Muslim. Ignorance of rules is not an acceptable excuse according to the *Sharî'ah*. Those who do not care to learn such rules will be answerable to Allāh, and might be punished on the Day of Judgement.

It is therefore, extremely necessary for every Muslim to learn these details. May Allāh help us all.

Chapter:2

The Rules and Principles about Giving Name and Surname to the Children

- When should a Baby be Given a Name?
- What is the Criteria for Pleasant and Unpleasant Names?
- Teachings about the Selection of Names
- Teachings about Names and Surnames

When should a Baby be Given a Name?

Naming the neonate baby is a custom common to all mankind. In every society the parents select and give beautiful names to their children to be identified by the friends and relatives of the family. As Islām gives us guidance for every walk of life, it has appreciated the custom of giving good names to the children. Moreover, it has laid down some rules and principles which bring the issue in the limelight.

Islām has laid down these rules so that parents may be able to select a good and respectable name for the baby. Some of these are given below.

Naming a baby on the seventh day of its birth is a well-known practice but some of the sayings of the Prophet ﷺ indicate that naming a baby earlier is also lawful.

Samurah رضي الله عنه reports that the Messenger of Allāh ﷺ said:

«كُلُّ غُلَامٍ رَهِينَةٌ بِعَقِيقَتِهِ، تُذْبَحُ عَنْهُ يَوْمَ سَابِعِهِ وَيُحْلَقُ وَيُسَمَّى»

"The baby is pawned against 'Aqīqah which should be done on the seventh day and on that day the baby's head should be shaved and he should also be given a name."[1]

But there are also some other sayings of the Prophet ﷺ

[1] [Abū Dāwūd: 2838, Tirmidhi: 1522]

according to which a baby may be named earlier. Sahl bin Sa'd Sā'idī ﷺ says:

«أُتِيَ بِالْمُنْذِرِ بْنِ أَبِي أُسَيْدٍ إِلَى النَّبِيِّ ﷺ حِينَ وُلِدَ، فَوَضَعَهُ عَلَى فَخِذِهِ . . . وَأَبُوأُسَيْدٍ جَالِسٌ . . . فَلَهَا النَّبِيُّ ﷺ بِشَيْءٍ بَيْنَ يَدَيْهِ، فَأَمَرَ أَبُوأُسَيْدٍ بِابْنِهِ فَاحْتُمِلَ مِنْ فَخِذِ النَّبِيِّ ﷺ، فَاسْتَفَاقَ النَّبِيُّ ﷺ فَقَالَ: أَيْنَ الصَّبِيُّ؟ فَقَالَ أَبُوأُسَيْدٍ: قَلَبْنَاهُ يَارَسُولَ اللهِ! قَالَ: مَا اسْمُهُ؟ قَالَ: فُلَانٌ، قَالَ: وَلَكِنِ اسْمُهُ الْمُنْذِرُ»

"When Al-Mundhir bin Abū 'Usaid was born, he was brought to the Prophet ﷺ who placed him on his thigh. While Abū Usaid was sitting there, the Prophet ﷺ was busy with something in his hands so Abū Usaid told someone to take his son from the thigh of the Prophet ﷺ. When the Prophet ﷺ finished his job (with which he was busy), he said: "Where is the boy?" Abū Usaid replied, "We have sent him home." The Prophet ﷺ said, "What is his name?" Abū Usaid said, "(His name is) so and so." The Prophet ﷺ said, "No, his name is Al-Mundhir."[1]

From that day the boy was called as Al-Mundhir.

Anas ﷺ reported that the Messenger of Allāh ﷺ said:

«وُلِدَ لِيَ اللَّيْلَةَ غُلَامٌ، فَسَمَّيْتُهُ بِاسْمِ أَبِي، إِبْرَاهِيمَ»

"A son was born to me tonight and I have named him Ibrāhīm after my ancestor Ibrāhīm ﷺ."[2]

---

[1] [Bukhārī: 619, Muslim: 2149]

[2] [Muslim: 2315]

Summary:

The saying of the Prophet ﷺ quoted above shows that there is relaxation about the time of naming the baby. The name may be given on the first day, or it may be delayed till *'Aqīqah* (the seventh day) and even after that.

Desirable and the Undesirable Names

It is obligatory for the parents, guardians and elders of the family to select an excellent and meaningful name for the baby that should be appreciated by every learned person. Our beloved Prophet ﷺ also advised and urged to give meaningful names to the children.

The Best Names:

Ibn Umar رضي الله عنهما narrated that the Prophet ﷺ said:

«إِنَّ أَحَبَّ أَسْمَائِكُمْ إِلَى اللهِ عَبْدُاللهِ وَعَبْدُالرَّحْمٰنِ»

"Surely Allāh likes two of your names, 'Abdullah and 'Abdur Rahmān."[1]

Undesirable and Evil Names:

Islāmic *Sharî'ah* is pure, explicit and clear in all aspects. Like all other fields of life, it has laid down certain rules for naming the child and it forbids giving bad names to them. The *Sharî'ah* also stops from giving bad name to the child and applying such names which are unbecoming for the Islāmic personality, against his dignity or the Islāmic culture and society.

Of the Undesirable and Evil Names

The undesirable and bad names may be of the following

[1] [Muslim: 2132]

six types. We are going to give them in detail so that Muslims should learn and refrain from adopting any of them:

1. The parents and guardians should avoid giving ridiculous and evil names to the baby so that it should not be satired or dishonored at any place or time. 'Āishah ﵂ narrated:

«أَنَّ النَّبِيَّ ﷺ كَانَ يُغَيِّرُ الِاسْمَ الْقَبِيحَ»

"The Prophet ﷺ used to replace bad names."[1]

'Abdullah bin 'Umar ﵄ narrated:

«أَنَّ ابْنَةً لِعُمَرَ كَانَتْ يُقَالُ لَهَا عَاصِيَةُ، فَسَمَّاهَا رَسُولُ اللهِ ﷺ جَمِيلَةَ»

"The Prophet ﷺ had replaced the name عَاصِيَةُ ['Āsiah] the daughter of Umar ﵁ with جَمِيله [Jamīlah], because 'Āsiah means, 'Sinful' whereas Jamīlah means 'Beautiful'.[2]

Imām Abū Dāwūd said that the Prophet ﷺ had replaced the following names:

اَلْعَاص [Al-'Āas] "Disobedient", عَزِيْز ['Azīz] "Mighty, great", ('Azīz is the attribute of Allāh), عَتَلَه ['Atalah] "Rough, hard" شَيْطَان [Shaitān] 'Satan', the outcast", اَلْحَكَم [Al-Hakam] "The Supreme Judge", غُرَاب [Ghurāb] "A certain black bird, or crow", حُبَاب [Hubāb] "A serpant, a devil". The Prophet ﷺ replaced the name شِهَاب [Shihāb] "Flame, or brand" with هِشَام [Hishām] "Generosity", حَرب [Harb] "War, fighting" with سِلْم [Silm] "Peace and security", مُضْطَجِع [Mudtaji'] "Prostrate" with مُنْبَعِث

[1] [Tirmidhaī: 2839, Sahīhah: 207]

[2] [Muslim: 2139, Tirmidhī: 2828]

[Mumbaith] "Rising", عفِر ['Afirah] "Barren land" with خضِرا [Khadirah] "Verdant, fertile",شِعَبُ الضَّلَالَة [Shi'b-ud-Dalālah] "Valley of error" with شِعْبُ الْهُدٰى [Shi'b-ul-Hudā] "Valley of guidance", بَنُوالزِّنْيَه [Banū Zinyah] "Bastard" with بَنُوالرِّشْدَة [Banū-ar-Rishdah] "The rightly guided", and بَنُومُغْوِيه [Banū Mughviyah] "Misguided" with بَنُو رِشْد [Banū Rishdah]. Imām Abū Dāwūd ﷺ says that he had omitted the sources of such *Ahādīth* for the sake of brevity.[1]

2. Every believer should avoid ominous names so that the baby may be safe from their harm, because the person may be known as an ill omen. In this regard we quote the following *Hadīth*.

Sa'īd bin Musayyab ﷺ narrated from his father who visited the Prophet ﷺ. The Prophet ﷺ asked him:

«أَنَّ أَبَاهُ جَاءَ إِلَى النَّبِيِّ ﷺ فَقَالَ: مَا اسْمُكَ؟ قَالَ: حَزْنٌ، قَالَ: أَنْتَ سَهْلٌ، قَالَ: لَا أُغَيِّرُ اسْمًا سَمَّانِيهِ أَبِي، قَالَ ابْنُ الْمُسَيَّبِ: فَمَا زَالَتِ الْحُزُونَةُ فِينَا بَعْدُ»

"What is your name?" He said: "My name is حَزْن [Hazn] "Grief and mourning", the Prophet ﷺ said: "Your name should be سَهل [Sahl] "Easy, soft and smooth." He said: "I shall not change the name with which my father has named me." Sa'īd bin Musayyab ﷺ added: "We had roughness (in character) ever since" and Grief, mourning and anxiety

[1] [Abū Dāwūd: 4956]

became a part of our home, after the incident.[1]

Yahyā bin Sa'id رحمه الله says:

«أَنَّ عُمَرَ بْنَ الْخَطَّابِ قَالَ لِرَجُلٍ: مَا اسْمُكَ؟ فَقَالَ جَمْرَةُ، فَقَالَ ابْنُ مَنْ؟ فَقَالَ: ابْنُ شِهَابٍ، قَالَ: مِمَّنْ؟ قَالَ: مِنَ الْحُرْقَةِ، قَالَ: أَيْنَ مَسْكَنُكَ؟ قَالَ: بِحَرَّةِ النَّارِ، قَالَ بِأَيِّهَا؟ قَالَ: بِذَاتِ لَظًى، قَالَ عُمَرُ: أَدْرِكْ أَهْلَكَ فَقَدِ احْتَرَقُوا، قَالَ فَكَانَ كَمَا قَالَ عُمَرُ بْنُ الْخَطَّابِ رَضِيَ اللهُ عَنْهُ»

'Umar bin Khattāb رضي الله عنه asked a man: "What is your name?" he said: جَمْرَ [Jamrah], "A burning piece of coal." 'Umar said, "What is the name of your father?" He said: شِهَاب [Shihāb] "Son of a flame". He asked: "What is the name of your tribe?" he said: حُرْقه [Hurqah] "Burnt in fire." 'Umar asked: "Where do you live?" he said: "inحَرَّةُ النَّار [Harra-tun-Nar] "An area of fire". 'Umar رضي الله عنه again asked: "In which valley?" he said: " ذَاتُ لَظٰى [Dhāt Lazā] "Valley of flames." 'Umar رضي الله عنه said: "Then rush to save your family, fire has burnt them to ashes." "The narrator of this event says that his house and family were really burnt to ashes as' Umar رضي الله عنه had said."[2]

3. It is a law of *Sharī'ah* to avoid such names as اَلْاَحَدُ [Al-'Ahad], اَلصَّمَدُ [As-Samad], اَلرَّزَّاقُ [Ar-Razzāq] as they are particular to Allāh The Almighty, however, it is quite appropriate to place the word عَبد as prefix to Allāh's divine attribute and

[1] [Bukhārī: 6190]

[2] [Muwatta Imām Mālik:1871]

name a baby then. Hānī ﷺ says:

«إِنَّهُ لَمَّا وَفَدَ إِلَى رَسُولِ اللهِ ﷺ مَعَ قَوْمِهِ، سَمِعَهُمْ يُكَنُّونَهُ بِأَبِي الْحَكَمِ، فَدَعَاهُ رَسُولُ اللهِ ﷺ فَقَالَ: إِنَّ اللهَ هُوَ الْحَكَمُ وَإِلَيْهِ الْحُكْمُ، فَلِمَ تُكَنَّى أَبَا الْحَكَمِ؟ فَقَالَ: إِنَّ قَوْمِي إِذَا اخْتَلَفُوا فِي شَيْءٍ أَتَوْنِي فَحَكَمْتُ بَيْنَهُمْ، فَرَضِيَ كِلَا الْفَرِيقَيْنِ، فَقَالَ رَسُولُ اللهِ ﷺ: مَا أَحْسَنَ هٰذَا فَمَالَكَ مِنَ الْوَلَدِ؟ قَالَ: لِي شُرَيْحٌ وَمُسْلِمٌ وَعَبْدُاللهِ، قَالَ: فَمَنْ أَكْبَرُهُمْ؟ قَالَ: قُلْتُ: شُرَيْحٌ قَالَ: فَأَنْتَ أَبُوشُرَيْحٍ»

"Hānī ﷺ quoted his father as saying that when he went with his people on a deputation to the Messenger of Allāh ﷺ, he heard them calling him by the surname أبُوالحَكَم [Abū-al-Hakam]. So the Messenger of Allāh ﷺ called him and said: Allāh is الْحَكَم [Al-Hakam] as He is "The Supreme Judge and He rules with justice, and makes all the decisions". The Prophet ﷺ asked: Why are you addressed with the surname "أبُوالحَكَم"? He replied: The people called him 'Al-Hakam' because they brought their disputes to him for judgment and accepted his decisions. The Messenger of Allāh ﷺ said: "It is an excellent work, but how many children have you?" He said: "I have three, Shuraih, Muslim and 'Abdullāh." The Prophet ﷺ asked: "Who is the eldest of them." Hānī said: "Shuraih is the eldest." The prophet ﷺ said: "Then your surname is Abū Shuraih from now onwards."[1]

[1] [Abū Dāwūd: 4955 Nasā'ī: 5389, Irwā': 2615]

Abū Hurairah ﷺ narrated that the Prophet ﷺ said:

«أَغْيَظُ رَجُلٍ عَلَى اللهِ يَوْمَ الْقِيَامَةِ، وَأَخْبَثُهُ وَأَغْيَظُهُ عَلَيْهِ، رَجُلٌ كَانَ يُسَمَّى مَلِكَ الْأَمْلَاكِ، لَا مَلِكَ إِلَّا اللهُ»

"On the Day of Judgment the most detested and cursed person will be he who got himself called مَلِكُ الأَمْلَاك [Malik-ul-'Amlāk] "The king of kings", مَلِك [Mālik] is none except than Allāh, The Almighty."[1]

4. The believers should also avoid names which imply the meanings of prosperity, blessing, etc. Because if somebody asks about that person and he is not at home, the answer will be, "Not in the house." For example, if somebody asks, "يَسار [Yasār] "Blessing" at home?" And the reply will be 'Not in the house'. It is a negation of blessing for that house. Similarly there are certain names like أَفْلَح [Aflah] "Successful" نافع [Nāfi'] "Profitable" رَبَاح [Rabāh] "Useful" and نَجِيح [Najīh] "Successful" should also be abandoned.

Samurah bin Jundub ﷺ narrated that the Messenger of Allāh ﷺ said:

«أَحَبُّ الْكَلَامِ إِلَى اللهِ أَرْبَعٌ: سُبْحَانَ اللهِ، وَالْحَمْدُ لِلهِ، وَلَا إِلَهَ إِلَّا اللهُ، وَاللهُ أَكْبَرُ، لَا يَضُرُّكَ بِأَيِّهِنَّ بَدَأْتَ، لَا تُسَمِّيَنَّ غُلَامَكَ يَسَارًا، وَلَا رَبَاحًا، وَلَا نَجِيحًا، وَلَا أَفْلَحَ، فَإِنَّكَ تَقُولُ: أَثَمَّ هُوَ؟ فَلَا يَكُونُ، فَيَقُولُ: لَا، إِنَّمَا هُنَّ أَرْبَعٌ فَلَا تَزِيدُنَّ عَلَيَّ»

[1] [Muslim: 2143]

"The best words to Allāh are: سُبْحَانَ اللّٰه [*Subhān Allāh*] "Allāh is free from imperfection," and اَلْحَمْدُ لله [*Al-Hamd-u-lillāh*] "All praises and thanks be to Allāh," لَا اِلٰهَ اِلَّااللّٰه [*Lā Ilāha illallāh*] "There is no true God except Allāh", and اللّٰهُ اكبر [*Allāhu-Akbar*] "Allāh is All Great," and it does not matter by which you start. And do not give your slave the names يَسَار [Yasār], رَبَاح [Rabāh], نَجِيح [Najīh], اَفْلَح [Aflah], as you may call him so and he would not be (as named) they are four and do not ask me more."[1]

Samurah bin Jundub ﷛ says:

«نَهٰى رَسُولُ اللهِ ﷺ أَنْ نُسَمِّيَ رَقِيقَنَا أَرْبَعَةَ أَسْمَاءٍ: أَفْلَحُ وَنَافِعٌ وَرَبَاحٌ وَيَسَارٌ»

"The Prophet ﷺ forbade us to name our slaves with any of these four names: اَفْلَح [Aflah], نَافع [Nāfi‘], رَبَاح [Rabāh] and يَسَار [Yasār]."[2]

5. The believers in Allāh and His Prophet ﷺ should not place the word عَبْد [‘Abd] as a prefix to any name other than Allāh, The Almighty, as in the forthcoming names, عَبْدُالْعُزّٰى [‘Abdul ‘Uzzā] "Slave of ‘Uzzā" or عَبْدُالْكَعْبَة [‘Abdul Ka‘bah] "Slave of the Ka‘bah" or عَبْدُالنَّبِى [Abdun Nabī] "Slave of the Prophet" are not allowed to be used. The Muslims should know that it is unlawful to use any of them.

Objection:

Some people may object that if such names are not allowed,

---

[1] [Muslim: 2137, ‘Abū Dāwūd: 4958]

[2] [Abū Dawud: 4958, Ibn Mājah: 3730]

then why did the Prophet ﷺ utter the following words in the Battle of Hunain against the unbelievers:

أَنَا النَّبِيُّ لَا كَذِبْ، أَنَا ابْنُ عَبْدِالْمُطَّلِبْ»

"I am the Prophet of Allāh without a lie, I am the son of 'Abdul Muttalib"[1]

Why did the Prophet ﷺ utter the name of his grandfather with عبد['Abd] which means "Slave of Muttalib?"

Answer:

'Allāmah Ibn Qayyim رحمه الله replies that the Prophet ﷺ forbids giving such names to babies. Uttering the name of a person known by that name is not violation of the rule." That is why the Prophet ﷺ never forbade his devoted followers from uttering the names of well known tribes like بنوعبد شمس [Banū-'Abd-Shams], بنوعبد الدار [Banū 'Abduddār] etc., which were adopted by those tribes before the advent of Islām.

To sum up, the popular name, even if it is un-Islāmic may be uttered for reference and introduction.

6. The Muslims should also be aware of all such names that are contrary to the Islāmic values, honor and dignity of human being, or those resembling to the pagans and unbelievers, and the names implying curse or ruin as: هيام [Hayām] "Lunatic". هَيْفَاء [Haifā'], " Slim, slender of waist" سَوْسَن [Sausan] "Lily", مَيادَة [Mayādah] "To move side to side." نَارِيمَان [Nārīmān] "A woman of brilliant face and bright body", أَحْلَام ['Ahlām] "Dream, vision."

[1] [Bukhārī: 2864, Muslim: 1776]

Philosophy of Good and Bad Names:

Bad and disgraceful names are forbidden in order to maintain the dignity of the Muslim *Ummah*, and to distinguish it from other nationalities. Islāmic norms and values should be reflected by names as a strong and dignified faith and respectable life style is all the more necessary in the present age in which the enemies of Islām never fail to degrade the Muslims and defame Islām. We should, therefore, be watchful against the enemies who are always looking for opportunities to ridicule, defame and destroy Islām by creating disunity and distrust among the Muslims. We should be united, avoid the sinful ways of life, and follow the excellent *Sunnah* of the Prophet ﷺ. We ask Allāh to help and guide us in every phase of individual and collective life.

Looking at the waywardness of the Muslims and prevailing un-Islāmic norms in their societies, seems quite appropriate that the Prophet ﷺ stressed upon his followers to stick to the sublime values of Islām by giving beautiful names of the Prophets عليهم السلام to the children.

A Comprehensive *Hadīth* about Names:

The Prophet ﷺ emphasized upon his companion to give either Prophets' names to the children or such names which imply the meaning of worship, humbleness towards Allāh Almighty. Abū Wahab Jashmi رضي الله عنه narrated:

«تَسَمَّوْا بِأَسْمَاءِ الْأَنْبِيَاءِ، وَأَحَبُّ الْأَسْمَاءِ إِلَى اللهِ: عَبْدُاللهِ وَعَبْدُالرَّحْمٰنِ، وَأَصْدَقُهَا حَارِثٌ وَهَمَّامٌ، وَأَقْبَحُهَا حَرْبٌ وَمُرَّةٌ»

"Name after the Prophets عليهم السلام and the most dearest names to Allāh are عَبدُالله ['Abdullāh] and عبدُالرّحمن ['Abdur Rahmān] and the most truthful of them are حَارث[Hārith] " Ploughman" and هَمَّام [Hammām], "Energetic, greatly solicitous about others." The worst are حَرْب [Harb] "War" and مُرَّة[Murrah] "Bitter"[1]

Surely by following all commandments of the Prophet ﷺ, including this advice, the Muslim *Ummah* will become the best nation in the world and it would dominate all others. Also it will serve as a beacon of light to show the right path (Islāmic way of life) to the world.

[1] [Abū Dāwūd: 4950, Musnad Ahmad: 4/345, Irwa': 1178, Sahihah: 1040]

The Rules and Principles for Giving *Kunyah* (Surname)

One of the measures related to naming a child is giving it a title or name of honor, known as *Kunyah* (surname). Sayings of the Prophet ﷺ also bear out the custom of giving *Kunyah* (surname) to the children. There are many logical reasons and advantages, some of these are given below.

❖ It is hoped that the surname may enable the child to adopt the excellent manners and would be a man of noble character. The *Kunyah* (surname) develops self-respect in the child, and inspires him to become a respectable member of the society. It is also hoped that *Kunyah* improves the child from the moral point of view, and helps him to become a useful member of the Muslim society. A poet says in a verse:

أُكَـنِّيهِ حِـينَ أُنَادِيهِ لِأُكْرِمَهُ

وَلَا أُلَقِّبُهُ وَالـسَّـوْءَةُ اللَّقَبُ

"I address him with a surname to honor him
And I avoid to entitle him as it is unbefitting."[1]

[1] [Tuhfat-ul-Moudūd, page: 127]

Importance of Giving Surname to a Child according to Sharī'ah

The Prophet ﷺ used to address children by their *Kunyah* so that their parents might know the importance of the *Kunyah*. We should also follow this noble example of our beloved guide and leader, Prophet Muhammad ﷺ in order to be richly blessed by Allāh.

Anas رضي الله عنه narrated:

«كَانَ النَّبِيُّ ﷺ أَحْسَنَ النَّاسِ خُلُقًا، وَكَانَ لِي أَخٌ يُقَالُ لَهُ: أَبُوعُمَيْرٍ، قَالَ: أَحْسِبُهُ فَطِيمًا، وَكَانَ إِذَا جَاءَ قَالَ: يَاأَبَا عُمَيْرٍ! مَا فَعَلَ النُّغَيْرُ؟ نُغَيْرٌ كَانَ يَلْعَبُ بِهِ»

"The Prophet ﷺ was the best of all the people in character. I had a brother called Abū 'Umair who, I think, had been newly weaned. Whenever he (that child) was brought to the Prophet ﷺ, he used to say: "Abū 'Umair' what did An-Nu-Ghair (nightingale) do?" It was a nightingale with which he used to play."[1]

[1] [Bukhārī: 6203, Muslim: 2150]

Practice of the Companions of the Prophet ﷺ

The surname brings the personality of a child to the limelight and inspires him to struggle for a noble position in the society. The Prophet ﷺ allowed 'Āishah ؓ to adopt the surname ام عبدالله Umm 'Abdullāh, although 'Abdullāh bin Zubair ؓ was the son of 'Ā'ishah's sister, Asmā bint Abū Bakr ؓ."[1]

Anas ؓ was known by the surname, ابوحمزه "Abū Hamzah", although he had no child.

Abū Hurairah ؓ was known by his surname although his real name was 'Abdur Rahmān and he had no child.

Any other *Kunyah* with reference to one's child may be adopted even by those who do not have children. A few examples are given below:

Abū Bakr ؓ had no son named بكر [Bakr] but he is known by this surname.

'Umar ؓ was known by the surname ابوحفص [Abū Hafs], although he had no son named "Hafs".

Abū Dhar Ghiffāri ؓ had no son named ذر [Dhar], but he is known by his surname.

Khalid bin Walîd's surname was ابوسليمان [Abū Sulaiman],

---

[1] [Abū Dāwūd: 4970, Sahīhah: 132]

although he had no son named "Sulaimān".[1]

Several other instances may be cited for giving surnames. From the facts and references given above we can conclude that giving a *Kunyah* (surname) to a child is a practice approved by the Prophet ﷺ. The surname may be adopted even by the adults. The *Kunyah* may not necessarily refer to the name of the person's child, and even the childless people are allowed to adopt a surname.

[1] [Tuhfat-ul-Moudūd, page: 127]

Miscellaneous Rules and Principles about Name, Title and Surname

How to resolve the issue if the parents differ about giving a certain name to a child:

If the father and mother differ about the name of their child, then the father's view should be preferred because giving a name to the child is the responsibility of the father. Several sayings of the Prophet ﷺ bear out the fact, and the Holy Qur'ān makes it clear that the child will be known with reference to his father, not with his mother. Allāh Almighty says:

﴿ٱدْعُوهُمْ لِءَابَآئِهِمْ هُوَ أَقْسَطُ عِندَ ٱللَّهِ﴾

"Call them (adopted sons) by the name of their fathers: that is more just with Allāh."[1]

There is a popular saying of the Prophet ﷺ already cited, makes it clear that the father of a child will give him a name.

Anas رضي الله عنه narrated that the Messenger of Allāh ﷺ said:

«وُلِدَ لِيَ اللَّيْلَةَ غُلَامٌ، فَسَمَّيْتُهُ بِاسْمِ أَبِي، إِبْرَاهِيمَ»

"Tonight a son was born to me and I have named him, Ibrāhīm after my father (the Prophet Ibrāhīm عليه السلام)."[2]

---

[1] [Al-Ahzāb 33:5]

[2] [Muslim: 2315, Abū Dāwūd: 3126]

Bad Names and Titles

It is prohibited for parents as well as others to give a bad name to a child or address him with unbefitting titles, such as: "O wicked! O sinner! O Thugee, etc."

The Holy Qur'ān says:

﴿وَلَا تَنَابَزُوا بِالْأَلْقَابِ﴾

"And neither shall you defame one another by nicknames."[1]

Adopting the Name and Surname of the Prophet ﷺ:

The scholars are unanimous about adopting the Prophet's names or to give them to the children, is lawful. Jābir ﵁ narrated:

«وُلِدَ لِرَجُلٍ مِنَّا غُلَامٌ، فَسَمَّاهُ مُحَمَّدًا، فَقَالَ لَهُ قَوْمُهُ: لَا نَدَعُكَ تُسَمِّي بِاسْمِ رَسُولِ اللهِ ﷺ، فَانْطَلَقَ بِابْنِهِ حَامِلَهُ عَلَى ظَهْرِهِ، فَأَتَى بِهِ النَّبِيَّ ﷺ، فَقَالَ: يَارَسُولَ اللهِ! وُلِدَ لِي غُلَامٌ، فَسَمَّيْتُهُ مُحَمَّدًا، فَقَالَ لِي قَوْمِي: لَا نَدَعُكَ تُسَمِّي بِاسْمِ رَسُولِ اللهِ ﷺ، فَقَالَ رَسُولُ اللهِ ﷺ: تَسَمَّوْا بِاسْمِي وَلَا تَكْتَنُوا بِكُنْيَتِي، فَإِنَّمَا أَنَا قَاسِمٌ، أَقْسِمُ بَيْنَكُمْ»

"A baby was born to a man, one from our people, he named him Muhammad (after the Prophet ﷺ) and his people said: "We will not let you name him by the name of the Messenger of Allāh ﷺ, the man took his infant to his back and went to the Prophet ﷺ and said:O Messenger of Allāh!

[1] [Al-Hujurāt 49:11]

A baby was born to me and I named him Muhammad but my people said: "We will not allow to give him the name of the Messenger of Allāh ﷺ". The Messenger of Allāh ﷺ said: "Name yourselves by my name but not by my *Kunyah* (surname), because I am Qāsim as I only allot your shares".[1]

'Alī رضي الله عنه reports that he asked the Prophet ﷺ:

«قُلْتُ: يَارَسُولَ اللهِ! إِنْ وُلِدَ لِي مِنْ بَعْدِكَ وَلَدٌ أُسَمِّيهِ بِاسْمِكَ وَأُكَنِّيهِ بِكُنْيَتِكَ؟ قَالَ: نَعَمْ»

"I said O Allāh's Messenger ﷺ! Could I name my son, if I have one, after your name and use your surname after your demise? He said: "Yes".[2]

In his book "*Kitab-ul-Aadāb*", Hameed bin Zanjawiyah writes that he asked Ibn Abū Uwais: "Did Imām Mālik allow people to use the name and surname of the Prophet ﷺ?" 'Uwais pointed to a man sitting in the company and said: This is Muhammad bin Mālik, sitting by his side. His father, Imām Mālik named him محمد "Muhammad" and gave him the surname ابو القاسم "Abū-al-Qāsim." He also said that Imām Mālik used to say that combining the name and surname of the Prophet ﷺ was not allowed during the Prophet's lifetime, to avoid the confusion of identity. But now, after the demise of the Prophet ﷺ, it is allowed because there can be no confusion of identity with the Prophet ﷺ.

---

[1] [Bukhārī: 3114, Muslim: 2133]

[2] [Abū Dāwūd: 4967, Tirmidhī: 2843]

Anyway, adopting the name and surname of the Prophet ﷺ is permissible now a days.

For Parents and Guardians

Keeping in mind the teachings of Islām and instructions about giving certain names to the children and abandoning others, it becomes clear that parents should select excellent names for their children. They should give good titles and adopt noble surnames.

The children of today are the parents of the future, so they should be given such meaningful names that they should feel honor and dignity for their good names. Therefore, the parents should be careful about addressing the children with evil names so that they should not suffer from any inferiority complex. The parents are responsible for building the character of their offspring, as they are the immediate following generation. The parents, therefore, should build up the character of their children and make them useful members of the society but also bring peace and harmony in the society.

Allāh Almighty is Kind and Merciful Who sent the last and merciful Prophet Muhammad ﷺ as a model for the Muslims to follow. The Prophet ﷺ led us to Allāh's unbounded mercy. If we follow *Sunnah* of the Prophet ﷺ about naming the children and building up their characters, we shall be able to present a noble society, excellent generation of Islām and the members of excellent characters.

The surname would influence the social aspect of the child's character and by this he is expected to make effort to reach the exalted position of the elders.

Chapter:3

Allāh's Beautiful Names

- The Beautiful Names of Allāh mentioned in the Holy Qur'ān and *Hadīth*
- Meanings of Allāh's Beautiful Names
- References

Attributive Names of Allāh Almighty

The Messenger of Allāh ﷺ asked his followers to name their children after the Prophets عليهم السلام and the excellent Attributive Names of Allāh Almighty. It is quite appropriate to place any of the given words as a prefix to any of Allāh's Attributive Names and be given to the children. These words are:شمس، حمود، عبيد، مطيع، عبد، خليق، سيف، شاكر، ذاكر، قمر، نجم، سعيد ، حفيظ، شفيق، حميد عزيز، امين، خبيب، ساجد، منيب، اسد، مجيب، محب، فضل and etc.

Allāh (اللّٰه) [This is Allah's real Name and it is mentioned 2696 times in the Noble Qur'ān. (Al-Fātihah 1:1)]

Al-'Ahad (اَلْأَحَد) The One (only) [This attributive Name is mentioned only once in the Noble Qur'ān. (Al-'Ikhlās 112:1)]

Al-Ākhir (اَلْآخِر) The Last (of all), The Remainder when all will perish, [This attributive Name is mentioned only once in the Noble Qur'ān. (Al-Hadīd 57:3)]

Al-'A'lā (الأَعليٰ)The Most High [This is Allāh's attributive Name, and it is mentioned 2 times in the Noble Qur'ān. (Al-'A'la 187:1)]

Al-'Ilāh (اَلْإِلٰه) The Worshipped [This is Allah's most frequently mentioned attributive Name in the Noble Qur'ān. (Al-Baqarah 2:133)]

Al-'Awwal (اَلأَوَّل) The First of all, The First in the universe [This attributive Name is mentioned only once in the Noble Qur'ān. (Al-Hadīd 57:3)]

Al-Bārī (اَلْبَارِي) The Inventor [This attributive Name is mentioned 3 times in the Noble Qur'ān. (Al-Baqarah 2:54)]

Al-Bāsit (اَلْبَاسِط) The One Who amplifies [Tirmidhī: 3507, Ibn Mājah: 3861]

Al-Bātin (اَلْبَاطِن) The Most Near [This attributive Name is mentioned only once in the Noble Qur'ān. (Al-Hadīd 57:3)]

Al-Bā'ith (اَلْبَاعِث) The Sender, the Quickener of mankind

[Tirmidhi: 3507, Ibn Mājah: 3861]

Al-Badī' (اَلْبَدِيْع) The Originator [This attributive Name is mentioned 2 times in the Holy Qur'ān. (Al-Baqarah 2:117)]

Al-Bāqī (اَلْبَاقِي)The Everlasting [Tirmidhī: 3507]

Al-Barr (اَلْبَرّ) The Most Subtle, Kind [This attributive Name is mentioned only once in the Noble Qur'ān. (At-Tūr 52:28)]

At-Tawwāb(اَلتَّوَّاب) The Most Forgiving [This attributive Name is mentioned 11 times in the Noble Qur'ān. (Al-Baqarah: 2:37)]

Al-Basir(اَلْبَصِير) The All Seer [This attributive Name is mentioned 42 times in the Noble Qur'ān. (Al-Baqarah 2:96)]

Al-Jāmi' (اَلْجَامع) The Gatherer [This attributive Name is mentioned 2 times in the Noble Qur'ān. (Āl'Imrān 3:9)]

Al-Jabbār (اَلْجَبَّار) The Compeller [This attributive Name is mentioned only once in the Noble Qur'ān. (Al-Hashr 59:23)]

Al-Jalīl (اَلْجَلِيل) The Great, the Mighty [Tirmidhī: 3507]

Al-Hasīb (اَلْحَسِيب) The Account Taker [This attributive Name is mentioned 3 times in the Noble Qur'ān. (An-Nisā' 4:6)]

Al-Hafīz (اَلْحَفِيظ) The Watchful [This attributive Name is mentioned 3 times in the Noble Qur'ān. (Sabā 34:21)]

Al-Haqq (اَلْحَقّ) The Established, True [This attributive Name is mentioned 9 times in the Noble Qur'ān. (An-Nūr 24:2)]

Al-Hakam(اَلْحَكَم) The Judge, The Ruler [Abū Dāwūd: 4955, Tirmidhī: 3507]

Al-Hakīm (اَلْحَكِيم) The All Wise [This attributive Name is mentioned 94 times in the Holy Qur'ān. (Al-Baqarah 2:32)]

Al-Halīm (اَلْحَلِيم) The Most Forbearing [This attributive Name is mentioned 11 times in the Noble Qur'ān. (Al-Baqarah 2:257)]

Al-Hamīd (اَلْحَمِيد) The Worthy of All Praises [This attributive Name is mentioned 17 times in the Noble Qur'ān. (Al-Baqarah 2:267)]

Al-Hannān (اَلْحَنَّان) The Compassionate, the Affectionate [Musnad Ahmad 3:230]

Al-Hayy (اَلْحَيّ) The Ever-Living [This attributive Name is mentioned 5 times in the Noble Qur'ān. (Al-Baqarah 2:255)]

Hayiyyun (حَيِيٌّ) The Modest [Tirmidhī: 3556]

Al-Khāfid (اَلْخَافِض) The One Who is Humble, Who Humiliates [Tirmidhī:3507, Ibn Mājah: 3861]

Al-Khabīr (اَلْخَبِير) All Acquainted with [This attributive Name is mentioned 45 times in the Holy Qur'ān. (Al-Baqarah 2:234)]

Al-Khallāq (اَلْخَلَّاق) The Creator [This attributive Name is mentioned 2 times in the Holy Qur'ān. (Al-Hijr 15:86)]

Al-Khāliq (اَلْخَالِق) The Creator [This attributive Name is mentioned 8 times in the Holy Qur'ān. (Al-'An'ām 6:102)]

Ad-Dayyān (اَلدَّيَّان)The Requiter, Administrator, Ruler, Judge, [Bukhārī: 7481]

Dhu-al-Jalāli Wal-Ikrām(ذُوالْجَلَال والاِكْرَام) Full of Majesty and Honor [This attributive Name is mentioned 2 times in the Noble Qur'ān. (Ar-Rahmān 55:27)]

Dhu-Ar-Rahmah (ذُوالرَّحْمَة) Full of Mercy [This attributive Name has been mentioned 3 times in the Noble Qur'ān. (Al-'An'ām 6:133)]

Dhu-at-Taul (ذُوالطَّوْل) The Bestower [This attributive Name is mentioned only once in the Noble Qur'ān. (Al-Mu'min 40:15)]

Dhu-al-'Arsh (ذُوالْعَرْش) The Owner of the Throne [This attributive Name is mentioned 4 times in the Noble Qur'ān. (Al-Mu'min 40:15)]

Dhū-'Iqāb (ذُوعِقَاب) The Punisher [This attributive Name is mentioned only once in the Noble Qur'ān. (Fussilat 41:43)]

Dhū-al-Fadl (ذُوالْفَضْل) The Owner of Bounty [This attributive Name is mentioned 13 times in the Noble Qur'ān. (Al-Baqarah 2:105)]

Dhū-al-Quwwah (ذُوالْقُوَّة) The Owner of Power [This attributive Name is mentioned only once in the Noble Qur'ān. (Adh-Dhāriyāt

51:58)]

Dhū-al-Maghfirah (ذُوالمَغفْرَة)Full of Forgiveness [This attributive Name is mentioned 2 times in the Noble Qur'ān. (Ar-Ra'd 6:13)]

Ar-Rāfi' (اَلرَّافع) The Raiser [This attributive Name is mentioned only once in the Noble Qur'ān. (Āl'Imrān 3:55)]

Ar-Ra'ūf (اَلرَّؤُوف) The Most Kind [This attributive Name is mentioned 10 times in the Noble Qur'ān. (Al-Baqarah 2:143)]

Ar-Rabb(اَلرَّبّ) The Lord [This attributive Name is mentioned 968 times in the Noble Qur'ān. (Al-Fātihah 1:2)]

Ar-Rahmān (اَلرَّحْمٰن) The Most Compassionate [This attributive Name is mentioned 57 times in the Noble Qur'ān. (Al-Fātihah 1:1)]

Ar-Rahīm (اَلرَّحِيم) The Most Merciful [This attributive Name is mentioned 114 times in the Noble Qur'ān. (Al-Fātihah 1:1,3)]

Ar-Razzāq (اَلرَّزَّاق) The All Provider [This attributive Name is mentioned only once in the Noble Qur'ān. (Adh-Dhāriyāt 51:58)]

Ar-Rashīd (اَلرَّشِيد) The Rightly Guided [Tirmidhī: 3507]

Rafī'-ud-Darajāt (رَفِيعُ الدَّرَجَات) The Raiser of Ranks, [This attributive Name is mentioned only once in the Noble Qur'ān. (Al-Mu'min 40:15)]

Ar-Raqīb (اَلرَّقِيب) The All Watcher [This attributive Name is mentioned 3 times in the Noble Qur'ān. (An-Nisā' 4:1)]

Subhān (سُبْحَان) The Glorified [This attributive Name is mentioned 41 times in the Noble Qur'ān. (Yūsuf 12:108)]

Sittīr (سِتِّير) He Who Covers sins [Nasā'ī: 406]

As-Salām (اَلسَّلَام)The Giver of Security [This attributive Name is mentioned only once in the Holy Qur'ān. (Al-Hashr 59:23)]

As-Samī' (اَلسَّمِيع) The All Hearer [This attributive Name is mentioned 47 times in the Noble Qur'ān. (Al-Baqarah 2:127)]

Ash- Shāfī (اَلشَّافِي) He Who Recovers, Heals [Tirmidhī: 3419]

Ash-Shākir (اَلشَّاكِر) The All Thankful [This attributive Name is mentioned 2 times in the Noble Qur'ān. (Al-Baqarah 2:158)]

Ash-Shakūr (اَلشَّكُور) The Most Recognizer [This attributive Name is mentioned 4 times in the Noble Qur'ān. (Fātir 35:30)]

Ash-Shahīd (اَلشَّهِيد) The Witness [This attributive Name is mentioned 19 times in the Noble Qur'ān. (Āl'Imrān 3:98)]

As-Subūr (اَلصُّبُور)The Most Tolerant, Forbearing [Tirmidhī: 3507]

As-Samad (اَلصَّمَد) The Self Sufficient [This attributive Name is mentioned only once in the Noble Qur'ān. (Al-'Ikhlās 112:2)]

Ad-Dārr(اَلضَّار) The Harming, Hurting [Tirmidhī: 3507]

Az-Zāhir (اَلظَّاهِر) The Most High [This attributive Name is mentioned only once in the Noble Qur'ān. (Al-Hadīd 57:3)]

Al-'Adl (اَلْعَدْل) The Just, the Equitable [Tirmidhī: 3507]

Al-'Azīz (اَلْعَزِيز) The Almighty [This attributive Name is mentioned 89 times in the Noble Qur'ān. (Al-Baqarah 2:129)]

Al-'Azīm (اَلْعَظِيم) The Most Great [This attributive Name is mentioned 6 times in the Noble Qur'ān. (Al-Baqarah 2:255)]

Al-'Afuww(اَلْعَفُوّ) The Most Forgiving [This attributive Name is metioned only once in the Holy Qur'ān. (An-Nisā' 4:43)]

Al-'Allām(اَلْعَلَّام) The All Knower [This attributive Name is mentioned 4 times in the Noble Qur'ān. (Al-Mā'idah 5:109)]

Al-'Alīyy (اَلْعَلِيّ) The Most High [This attributive Name is mentioned 8 times in the Noble Qur'ān. (Al-Baqarah 2:255)]

Al-'Alīm (اَلْعَلِيم) The All Knower [This attributive Name is mentioned 153 times in the Noble Qur'ān. (Al-Baqarah 2:29,32,95)]

Al-Ghīfir (اَلْغَافِر) The Most Forgiving [This attributive Name is mentioned only once in the Noble Qur'ān. (Al-Mu'min 40:3)]

Al-Ghālib (اَلْغَالِب) The Victor, the Conqueror [This attributive Name is mentioned once in the Noble Qur'ān. (Yūsuf 12:21)]

Al-Ghaffār (اَلْغَفَّار)The Most Forgiving [This attributive Name is mentioned 5 times in the Noble Qur'ān. (Tāhā 20:82)]

Al-Ghafūr (اَلْغَفُور) The Forgiving [This attributive Name is mentioned 91 times in the Noble Qur'ān. (Al-Baqarah 2:173)]

Al-Ghaniyy(اَلْغَنِيّ) The Rich [This attributive Name is mentioned 18 times in the Noble Qur'ān. (Al-Baqarah 2:263)]

Al-Fātir(اَلْفَاطِر) The Creator [This attributive Name is mentioned 6 times in the Noble Qur'ān. (Al-'An'ām 6:14)]

Al-Fāliq (اَلْفَالِق) The Splitter [This attributive Name is mentioned 2 times in the Noble Qur'ān. (Al-'An'am 6:95)]

Al-Fattāh(اَلْفَتَّاح) The Opener, the Conqueror [This attributive Name is mentioned only once in the Noble Qur'ān. (Sabā 34:26)]

Al-Qābid (اَلْقَابِض) The Seizer, the Collector [Tirmidhī: 3507, Ibn-

Mājah: 3861]

Qābil-ut-Toub (قَابِلُ التَّوْب) The Acceptor of Repentance [This attributive Name is mentioned only once in the Noble Qur'ān. (Al-Mu'min 40:3)]

Al-Qādir (اَلْقَادِر) The All Powerful [This attributive Name is mentioned 7 times in the Noble Qur'ān. (Al-'An'ām 6:37)]

Al-Qādī (اَلْقَاضِي) The Judge [Tirmidhī: 3419]

Al-Qāhir (اَلْقَاهِر)The Omnipotent, the Almighty [This attributive Name is mentioned 2 times in the Noble Qur'ān. (Al-'An'ām 6:18, 61)]

Al-Quddūs (اَلْقُدُّوس) The Holy [This attributive Name is mentioned 2 times in Noble Qur'ān. (Al-Hashr 59:23)]

Al-Qarīb (اَلْقَرِيب) The Near, Close [This attributive Name is mentioned 3 times in the Noble Qur'ān. (Hūd 11:61)]

Al-Qawiyy (اَلْقَوِيّ) The Subduer of His Creatures by His Power [This attributive Name is mentioned 9 times in Noble Qur'ān. (Al-'Anfāl 8:52)]

Al-Qahhār (اَلْقَهَّار) The Irresistible [This attributive Name is mentioned 6 times in the Noble Qur'ān. (Yūsuf 12:39)]

Al-Qayyām (اَلْقَيَّام) The Self Existent, Everlasting [Bukhārī: 7442, Tirmidhī: 3418]

Al-Qayyim (اَلْقَيِّم)The Unchangeable, the Maintainer [Bukhārī: 1120, 7499]

Al-Qayyūm (اَلْقَيُّوم)The Eternal, Sustainer [This attributive Name is mentioned 3 times in the Noble Qur'ān. (Al-Baqarah 2:255)]

Al-Kabīr(اَلْكَبِيْر) The Most Great, the Majestic [This attributive Name is mentioned 6 times in the Noble Qur'ān. (Al- Hajj 22:62)]

Al-Karīm (اَلْكَرِيم) The Bountiful [This attributive Name is mentioned 3 times in the Noble Qur'ān. (An-Naml 27:40)]

Al-Kafīl (اَلْكَفِيل) The Guarantor, the Sponsor [This attributive Name is mentioned only once in the Noble Qur'ān. (An-Nahl 16:91)]

Al-Latīf (اَللَّطِيف) The Most Subtle and Courteous [This attributive Name is mentioned 7 times in the Noble Qur'ān. (Al-'An'ām 6:103)]

Al-Mājid (اَلْمَاجِد) The Glorious, the Illustrious [Tirmidhī: 3507, Ibn Mājah: 3861]

Al-Mālik (اَلْمَالِك) The King [This attributive Name is mentioned 2 times in the Noble Qur'ān. (Āl-'Imrān 3:26)]

Al-Māni' (اَلْمَانِع) The Prohibitor, the Forbidding [Tirmidhī: 3507 Ibn Mājah: 3861]

Al-Mu'akkhhir (اَلْمُؤَخِّر) The Last of all [Bukhārī: 6317]

Al-Mu'min(اَلْمؤمِن) The Giver of Security [This attributive Name is mentioned only once in the Noble Qur'ān. (Al-Hashr 59:23)]

Al-Mubdi'u (اَلْمُبْدِئُ) The Creator, One Who Commences [Tirmidhī: 3507, Ibn Mājah: 3861]

Al-Muta'āl (اَلْمُتَعَال) The Most High [This attributive Name is mentioned only once in the Noble Qur'ān. (Ar-Ra'd 13:9)]

Al-Mut'ālī(اَلْمُتَعَالِي) The Most High [Tirmidhī: 3507]

Al-Mutakabbir (اَلْمتكبِّر) The Compeller, the Supreme [This attributive Name is mentioned only once in the Noble Qur'ān. (Al-Hashr 59:23)]

Al-Mutawaffī (اَلْمُتَوَفِّي) He Who takes fully [This attributive Name is mentioned only once in the Noble Qur'ān. (Āl-'Imrān 3:55)]

Al-Matīn (اَلْمَتِيْن)The Most Strong, the Eternal [This attributive Name is mentioned only once in the Noble Qur'ān. (Adh-Dhāriyāt 51:58)]

Al-Mujīb (اَلْمُجيْب) The Ever Responding [This attributive Name is mentioned 7 times in the Noble Qur'ān. (Hūd 11:61)]

Al-Majīd(اَلْمجيْد) All Glorious, All Praiseworthy [This attributive Name is mentioned 2 times in the Noble Qur'ān. (Hūd 11:73, Al-Burūj 85:15)]

Al-Muhsī (اَلْمُحْصِي) He Who Comprehends Everything by His Knowledge [Tirmidhī: 3507]

Al-Muhyī (اَلْمُحْي) The Giver of Life, the Quickener [This attributive Name is mentioned 2 times in the Noble Qur'ān. (Fussilat 41:39)]

Al-Mukhrij (اَلْمُخْرج) He Who brings forth [This attributive Name is mentioned 3 times in the Noble Qur'ān. (Al-Baqarah 2:72)]

Al-Mukhzī (اَلْمخْزي) The Disgracer [This attributive Name is mentioned only once in the Noble Qur'ān. (At-Taubah 9:2)]

Al-Mudhillu (اَلْمُذِلُّ) The Humiliator [Tirmidhī: 3507, Ibn Mājah, *Hadīth*: 3861]

Al-Musawwir (اَلْمُصَوِّر)The Bestower of forms, [This attributive Name is mentioned only once in the Noble Qur'ān. (Al-Hashr 59:24)]

Al-Mu'izz(اَلْمُعِزّ) The Exalter [Tirmidhī: 3507, Ibn Mājah: 3861]

Al-Mu'tī (اَلْمُعْطِي) The Bestower, the Giver [Ibn Mājah: 3861]

Al-Mu'īd (اَلْمُعِيد) The Re-Creator [Tirmidhī: 3507, Ibn Mājah: 3861]

Al-Mughnī (اَلْمغْنِي) The Bestower, He Who Satisfies [Tirmidhī: 3507]

Al-Muqtadir (اَلْمقْتَدِر) The Owner of Majesty and Honor, He Who determines [This attributive Name is mentioned 3 times in the Noble Qur'ān. (Al-Qamar 54:42,55)]

Al-Muqaddim (اَلْمُقَدِّم) He Who makes things to go before [Bukhārī: 6317]

Al-Muqsit(اَلْمقْسِط) The Equitable [Tirmidhī: 3507]

Al-Malik (اَلْملك) The King, the Sovereign [This attributive Name is mentioned 5 times in the Noble Qur'ān. (Tāhā 20:114)]

Al-Muqīt (اَلْمقِيْت) The Giver of Sustenance [Tirmidhī: 3507]

Al-Malīk (اَلمليْك) The Omnipotent King, the Sovereign [This attributive Name is mentioned only once in the Noble Qur'ān. (Al-Qamar 54:55)]

Al-Mumīt (اَلْمُمِيْت)The Giver of Death [Tirmidhī: 3507]

Al-Mannān(اَلْمنَّان) The Most Generous, The Giver of all goods [Tirmidhī: 3544]

Al-Muntaqim(اَلْمُنْتَقِم) The Avenger [This attributive Name is derived from the word "ذُوانْتِقَام" which is mentioned 4 times in the Noble Qur'ān. (Tirmidhī: 3507)]

Al-Mun'im (اَلمنُعِم) The Bestower [This Name is derived from the word اَنعَمْتَ of Al-Fātihah 1:7]

Al-Munzil (اَلْمنزِل)The Revealer, the Bringer down [Tirmidhī: 3400]

Al-Muhaimin (اَلُمهَيْمِن) The Watcher over His Creatures [This attributive name is mentioned only once in the Noble Qur'ān. (Al-Hashr 59:23)]

Al-Muwaffī (اَلْمُوَفِّي) The One Who Gives and Takes fully [This attributive Name is mentioned only once in the Noble Qur'ān. (Hūd 11:109)]

An-Nasīr (اَلنَّصِير) The Helper, Protector, Patron [This attributive Name is mentioned 4 times in the Noble Qur'ān. (Al-Baqarah 2:107)]

An-Nūr(اَلنُّور) The Light [This attributive Name is mentioned 5 times in the Noble Qur'ān. (An-Nūr 24:35)]

Al-Hādī (اَلْهَادِي) The Guide, The Leader [Tirmidhī: 3507]

Al-Wārith (اَلْوَارِث) The Heir, One Who remains after the creatures [Tirmidhī: 3507]

Al-Wāhid(اَلْوَاحِد) The One, Unique [This attributive Name is mentioned 22 times in the Noble Qur'ān. (Al-Baqarah 2:133)]

Al-Wājid (اَلْوَاجِد) The Rich, He Who has no wants [Tirmidhī: 3507, Ibn Mājah: 3861]

Al-Wāsi‘ (اَلْوَاسِع) The Plentiful [This attributive Name is mentioned 9 times in the Noble Qur'ān. (Al-Baqarah 2:115)]

Al-Wālī (اَلْوَالِي)The Ruler, the King [Tirmidhī: 3507]

Al-Wahīd (اَلْوَحِيد) The Unique, Alone [This attributive Name is derived from the attributes: (اَلْاَحد) and (اَلْوَاحِد) so it seems correct]

Al-Wadūd (اَلْوَدُوْد) The Most Loving [This attributive Name is mentioned 2 times in the Noble Qur'ān. (Hūd 11:90, Al-Burūj 85:14)]

Al-Wakīl (اَلْوَكِيل) The Guardian [This attributive Name is mentioned 14 times in the Noble Qur'ān. (Āl'Imrān 3:173)]

Al-Waliyy (اَلْوَلِيّ) The Protector Guardian [This attributive Name is mentioned 15 times in the Noble Qur'ān. (Al-Baqarah 2:257)]

Al-Wahhāb (اَلْوَهَّاب) The Bestower, the Giver of gifts [This attributive Name is mentioned 3 times in the Noble Qur'ān. (Āl'Imrān 3:8)]

Chapter:4

This Chapter comprises on the names of the Noble Prophet Muhammad ﷺ, and names of the Male and Female companions of the last Prophet ﷺ in the following order:

- Names of the Messenger of Allah ﷺ
- The Noble Prophets عليهم السلام
- Wives of the Prophet رضي الله عنهن
- Children of the Prophet رضي الله عنهم
- The Rightly Guided Caliphs رضي الله عنهم
- The Ten Blessed Companions رضي الله عنهم
- The Martyrs of the Battle of Badr رضي الله عنهم
- The Participants of the Battle of Badr رضي الله عنهم
- The Eminent Male and Female Companions of the Prophet ﷺ
- Total Number of Names: 565

The excellent and authentic Names of the last Messenger of Allah ﷺ, the noble Prophets عليهم السلام, wives and children of the Prophet ﷺ have been given with their meanings and references. Amongst the Companions رضي الله عنهم, only names of the rightly guided caliphs, ten blessed Companions, martyrs of the Battle of Badr and its participants, and the names of several other eminent female Companions رضي الله عنهن have been given. The meanings of most of these names could be seen in chapters 5-6.

Names of the Messenger of Allah ﷺ

Ahmad (اَحْمَد) He who is most praised, commended, [This Name is mentioned only once in the Noble Qur'ān. (As-Saff 61:6)]

Amīn (امِين) The trusted, confided in, [This Name is mentioned only once in the Noble Qur'ān. (At-Takwīr 81:21)]

Al-Hāshir (اَلْحَاشِر) One who congregates, or collects the people together [Bukhārī: 3532]

Hirz (حِرْز) The guardian, protector [Bukhārī: 2125]

Harīs (حَرِيص) Excessively pitiful, compassionate [At-Taubah 9:128]

Al-Khātam (اَلْخَاتَم) The last of the Prophets عليهم السلام, [Al-'Ahzāb 33:40, Bukhārī: 3535]

Ad-dā'ī (اَلدَّاعِي) He who invites to Allāh. [Al-'Ahzāb: 33:46]

Rahmah (رَحْمَه) Mercy, pity [Al-'Anbiyā' 21:107]

Rahīm (رَحِيم) The compassionate, merciful [At-Taubah 9:128, Muslim: 2354]

Ra'ūf (رَ ؤُف) The pitiful [At-Taubah 9:128]

Sirājum-Munīr (سِرَاج مُنِير) The bright, illuminating lamp [Al-'Ahzāb 33:46]

Shāhid (شَاهِد) The witness [Al-'Ahzāb 33:45]

Shafī' (شَفِيْع)The intercessor [Muslim: 199]

Sādiq (صَادِق) The truthful [Bukhārī: 3332]

Al-'Āqib (اَلْعَاقِب) The coming after, last [Bukhārī: 3532]

Farat (فَرَط) One who proceeds, goes before. [Bukhārī: 6426]

Qāsim (قَاسِم) The distributor [Bukhārī: 3114]

Mubīn (مُبِيْن) The manifest, separating [Al-Hijr 15:89]

Mubashshir (مُبَشِّر)The bearer of glad tiding [Al-'Ahzāb 33:45]

Al-Māhī (اَلْمَاحى) The eliminator [Bukhārī: 3532]

Mutawakkil(مُتَوَكِّل) One who depends upon Allāh Almighty [Bukhārī: 2125]

Muhammad (مُحَمَّد) The praised, [This name is mentioned 4 times in the Noble Qur'ān. (Āl'Imrān 3:144)]

Mukhtār (مُخْتَار) Chosen, selected [Dārmī: 7]

Muddaththir (مُدَّثِّر)Wrapped in [Al-Mud-daththir 74:1]

Mudhakkir(مُذَكِّر) The reminder [Al-Ghāshiyah 88:21]

Muzzammil (مُزَّمِّل) Wrapped in [Al-Muzzammil 73:1]

Mushaffa'(مُشَفَّع) One whose intercession is accepted [Muslim: 2278]

Masdūq (مَصْدُوْق) The truly confirmed, inspired [Bukhārī: 3332]

Mustafā (مُصْطَفى) Chosen, selected [Musnad Ahmed:6/125]

Al-Muqaffī (اَلْمقفّى) One who comes last in succession [Muslim : 2355]

Mundhir(مُنْذِر) The warner [Ar-Ra'd 7:13]

Nabiyy-ut-Taubah (نَبِيُّ التَّوبَة)The Prophet of repentance [Muslim: 2355]

Nabi-ul-Malhamah (نَبِيُّ الْمَلْحَمَة) The Prophet of heroic battles [Musnad Ahmad: 4/395]

Nadhīr (نَذِيرْ) The warner [Al-Hajj 33:45]

Hādī (هَادِى) The guide, leader [An-Naml 27:81]

The Noble Prophets عليهم السلام

Ādam (آدَم) Dusky, dingy [This name is mentioned 25 times in the Noble Qur'ān. (Al-Baqarah 2:31)]

Ibrāhīm (اِبْرَاهِيْم) Servant [This name is mentioned 69 times in the Noble Qur'ān. (Al-Baqarah 2:124)]

Idrīs (اِدْرِيْس) Literate [This name is mentioned 2 times in the Noble Qur'ān. (Maryam 19:56)]

Īshāq (اِسْحَاق) Cheerful [This name is mentioned 17 times in the Noble Qur'ān. (Maryam 19:56)]

Ismā'īl (اِسْمَاعِيل) Joy, O Allāh! Listen [This name is mentioned 12 times in the Noble Qur'ān. (Al-Baqarah 2:125)]

Ilyās (اِلْيَاس) Firm, unwavering [This name is mentioned 3 times in the Noble Qur'ān. (Al-'An'ām 6:85)]

Ayyūb (اَيُّوب) The returning to Allāh [This name is mentioned 4 times in the Noble Qur'ān. (An-Nisā' 4:163)]

Dāwūd(دَاود) An Intimate friend [This name is mentioned 16 times in the Noble Qur'ān. (Al-Baqarah 2:251)]

Dhul-Kifl (ذُوالْكِفْل) He who is endowed with guarantee. According to most of the exegetes, he was a Prophet [This name is mentioned 2 times in the Noble Qur'ān. (Al-'Anbiyā' 21:85)]

Zakariyyā (زَكَرِيَّا) To fill a vessel [This name is mentioned 7 times in the Noble Qur'ān. (Āl'Imrān 3:37)]

Sulaimān (سُلَيْمَان) Peace, safety [This name is mentioned 17 times in the Noble Qur'ān. (Al-Baqarah 2:102)]

Shu'aib (شُعَيب) One who fills, repairs, [This name is mentioned 11 times in the Noble Qur'ān. (Al-'A'rāf 7:88)]

Shīth (شِيْث) Abundance [Tārīkh-At-Tabarī : 1/100]

Sālih (صَالِح) Pious, virtuous [This name is mentioned 9 times in the Noble Qur'ān. (Al-'A'rāf 7:77)]

'Uzair (عُزَيْر) To support, help, according to some of the exegetes, he was a Prophet [This name is mentioned 9 times in the Noble Qur'ān. (At-Taubah 9:30)]

'Īsā (عِيْسىٰ) Living [This name is mentioned 25 times in the Noble Qur'ān. (Al-Baqarah 2:87)]

Lūt (لُوْط) Hearty love and affection [This name is mentioned 27 times in the Noble Qur'ān. (Hūd 11:170)]

Muhammad (مُحَمَّد) The most praised [This name is mentioned 4 times in the Noble Qur'ān. (Āl'Imrān 3:144)]

Mūsā (مُوْسىٰ) Caught from water [This name is mentioned 136 times in the Noble Qur'ān. (Al-Baqarah 2:51)]

Nūh (نُوح) One who consoles [This name is mentioned 43 times in the Noble Qur'ān. (An-Nisā' 4:163)]

Hārūn (هارُون) Guardian, chief, commander [This name is mentioned 20 times in the Noble Qur'ān. (Al-Baqarah 2:248)]

Hūd (هُوْد) The Repentant [This name is mentioned 7 times in the Noble Qur'ān. (Hūd 11:53)]

Yahyā (يَحْيىٰ) The lasting, long lived [This name is mentioned 5 times in the Noble Qur'ān. (Āl'Imrān 3:39)]

Al-Yasa' (اليَسَع) Spacious [This name is mentioned 2 times in the Noble Qur'ān. (Al-'An'ām 6:86)]

Ya'qūb (يَعْقُوْب) The following, one who comes after [This name is mentioned 16 times in the Noble Qur'ān. (Al-Baqarah 2:132)]

Yūsuf (يُوسُف) Handsome, beautiful [This name is mentioned 37 times in the Noble Qur'ān. (Al-'An'ām 6:84)]

Yūsha' (يُوْشَع) Ascending, height [Bukhārī: 122]

Yūnus (يُوْنُس) Attracted, column, member [This name is mentioned 4 times in the Noble Qur'ān. (An-Nisā' 4:163)]

Names of the Wives ﷺ of the Prophet ﷺ

Khadījah bint Khuwailid (خَدِيْجَة بنت خويلد بن اسد) Incomplete [Marriage=15 years before the Prophethood]

Saudah bint Zam'ah (سَوْدَة بنت زمعه) Sign, Land of palm trees [Marriage=Shawwāl 10th year of Prophethood]

'Ā'ishah Siddiqah bint Abū Bakr Siddîq (عَائِشَه صديقه بنت ابوبكر صديق) Living [Marriage=Shawwal, 10th year of Prophethood]

Hafsah bint 'Umar Fārūq (حَفْصَة بنت عمر فاروق) Lioness [Marriage=3 AH]

Zainab bint Khuzaimah (زَيْنَب بنت خزيمه) Beautiful, fragrant plant [Marriage=4 AH.]

Umm Salamah Hind bint Abū Umayyah (اُمّ سَلَمه هِنْدبنت ابي اُمَيّه) Group [Marriage=Shawwal 4 AH]

Zainab bint Jahsh (زينَبْ بنت جَحْش) A beautiful fragrant plant [Marriage=Dhu-al-Qa'dah 5 AH]

Juwairiyah bint Hārith (جُوَيْرِيَه بنت حارث) A young lass [Marriage=Sha'bān 6 AH]

Ramlah, (Umm Habībah) bint Abū Sufyān (رَمْلَه (ام حبيبه) بنت ابي سفيان) Mound [Marriage=Muharram in 7 AH]

Safiyyah bint Huyayy bin Akhtab (صَفِيَّهْ بنت حيي بن اخطب)

Choice, pure [Marriage=7 AH]

Maimūnah bint Hārith (مَيْمُونَه بنت حارث) Blessed

[Marriage=Dhul-Qa'dah 7 AH]

Mariyah al-Qibtiyah bint Sham'ūn (ماريه القبطية بنت شمعون)

Female servant [Marriage=8 AH]

Jamīlah (جميله) Beautiful, handsome

Raihanah bint Zaid bin 'Amr (ريحانه بنت زيد بن عمرو) Patel flower, offspring [Marriage=5 AH]

Children of the Prophet ﷺ

Ibrāhīm (اِبْرَاهِيم) Servant [Zād ul Ma'ād : 1/103]

Umm Kulthūm (اُمِّ كُلْثُوم) Attractive [Zād ul Ma'ād : 1/103]

Ruqayyah (رُقَيَّة) Progress, development, height [Zād ul Ma'ād : 1/103]

Zainab (زَيْنَب) Beautiful [Zād ul Ma'ād: 1/103]

'Abdullāh (عَبْدُاللّٰه) Slave of Allāh [Zād ul Ma'ād: 1/103]

Fātimah (فَاطِمَة) Suckling woman, weaning or abactating [Zād ul Ma'ād: 1/103]

Qāsim (قَاسِم) Distributor [Zād-ul- Ma'ād: 1/103]

The Ten Blessed Companions ﷺ Who were Given the Glad Tiding of Paradise

Abū Bakr Siddīq 'Abdullāh bin 'Uthmān	ابوبكر صديق عبدالله بن عثمان
Abū Hafs 'Umar bin Al-Khattāb Al Fārūq	ابو حفص عمر بن الخطاب الفاروق
Abū 'Abdullāh 'Uthmān bin 'Affān	ابو عبدالله عثمان بن عفان
Abū-al- Hasan Alī bin Abū Tālib	ابوالحسن علي بن ابي طالب
Abū Muhammad Abdur Rahmān bin 'Auf	ابو محمد عبدالرحمٰن بن عوف
Abū Ishāq Sa'd bin Abū Waqqās	ابواسحاق سعد بن ابي وقاص
Abū Muhammad Talhah bin 'Ubaidullāh	ابو محمد طلحه بن عبيدالله
Abū 'Abdullah Zubair bin Al-'Awwām	ابو عبدالله زبير بن العوام
Abū-al-'Aa'war Sa'īd bin Zaid	ابوالأ عور سعيد بن زيد
Abū 'Ubaidah 'Āmir bin 'Abdullāh bin Al-Jarrāh	ابوعبيدة عامر بن عبدالله بن الجرّاح

The Martyrs of the Battle of Badr

‘Ammār bin Ziyād	عَمّار بن زياد
‘Āqil bin Bukair bin Abd Yālīl	عَاقِل بن بُكير بن عبدياليل
‘Auf or ‘Audh bin ‘Afrā’	عوف ياعَوْذ بن عفراء
Hārith or Hārithah bin Surāqah	حَارِث يا حارثه بن سراقه
Mihja‘ bin Sālih	مِهْجَع بن صالح
Mu‘awwidh bin ‘Afrā’	مُعَوِّذْ بن عفراء
Mubashshir bin ‘Abdul Mundhir	مُبَشِّرْ بن عبدالمنذر
Rāfi‘ bin Mu‘allā	رافع بن مُعَلّٰى
Sa‘d bin Khaithamah Al-’Ansārī	سَعْد بن خيثمه الأنصارى
‘Ubaidah bin Hārith bin Muttalib	عُبَيْدَه بن حارث بن مطلب
‘Umair bin ‘Abd ‘Umair	عُمَيْر بن عبد عمير
‘Umair bin Abū Waqqās	عُمَيْر بن ابي وقاص
‘Umair bin Humām	عُمَيْر بن حُمام
Yazīd bin Hārith	يَزِيْد بن حارث

The Participants of the Battle of Badr from the Emigrants

‘Abd Yālīl bin Nāshib Al-Laithī	عَبْدياليل بن ناشب الليثى
‘Abdullāh bin Asad bin Hilāl Al-Makhzūmī	عَبْدُاللّٰه بن اسد بن هلال المخزومى
‘Abdullāh bin Jahsh Al-’Asadī	عَبْدُاللّٰه بن جحش الأسدى
‘Abdullāh bin Makhramah	عَبْدُاللّٰه بن مخرمه
‘Abdullāh bin Maz‘ūn Al-Jumahī	عَبْدُاللّٰه بن مظعون الجمحي
‘Abdullāh bin Sa‘īd Al-’Umawī	عبداللّٰه بن سعيد الأموي
‘Abdullāh bin Suhail Al-‘Āmarī	عَبْدُاللّٰه بن سهيل العامري
‘Abdullāh bin Surāqah Al-‘Adawī	عَبْدُاللّٰه بن سراقه العدوي
‘Abdullāh bin Mas‘ūd Al-Hudhalī	عَبْدُاللّٰه بن مسعود الهذلي
‘Abdur Rahmān bin ‘Auf Az-Zuhrī	عَبْدُالرَّحْمٰن بن عوف الزهري
‘Abdur Rahmān bin Sahl Al-’Ansārī	عَبْدُالرَّحْمٰن بن سهل الأنصاري
Abū Bakr ‘Abdullāh bin ‘Uthmān As-Siddīq	ابوبكر عبداللّٰه بن عثمان الصِّدِّيق

Abū Hudhaifah bin 'Utbah	اَبُوحُذَيْفَه بن عتبه
Abū Kabshah (servant of the Messenger of Allāh ﷺ)	اَبُوكَبْشَه مولىٰ رسول اللّٰه
Abū Marthad Kināz bin Hasīn Al-Ghanawī	ابو مرثدكناز بن حصين الغنوي
Abū Sabrah bin Abū Ruham Al-Qurashī Al-'Āmarī	اَبُوسَبْرة بن ابي رُهم القرشي العامري
Abū Wāqid Hārith bin Mālik Al-Laithī	ابو وَاقِد حارث بن مالك الليثي
'Alī bin Abū Tālib Al-Murtadā	عَلِي بن ابي طالب المرتضىٰ
'Āmir bin 'Abdullāh Al-Qurashī	عَامِر بن عبداللّٰه القرشي
'Āmir bin Fuhairah Azdī	عَامِر بن فهيره ازدي
'Āmir bin Rabī'ah Al-'Anzī	عَامِر بن ربيعه العنزي
'Ammār bin Yāsir	عَمَّار بن ياسر
'Amr bin Abū 'Amr Al-Fihrī	عمْرو بن ابي عمرو الفهرى
'Amr bin Abū Sarh Al-Fihrī	عمْرو بن ابي سَرْح الفهري
'Amr bin Al-Hārith Al-Fihrī	عمرو بن الحارث الفهري
'Amr bin Surāqah Al-'Adawī	عَمْرو بن سراقه العدوي
'Amr or 'Āmir bin Hārith Al-Fihrī	عمْرويا عامر بن حارث الفِهري
'Āqil bin Bukair bin 'Abd Yālīl	عَاقِل بن بكير بن عبد ياليل
'Arqam bin Abul-'Arqam	اَرْقَم بن ابو الارقم

‘Auf bin Uthāthah Al-Muttalabī	عَوْف بن أُثاثه المطلبي
Bilāl bin Rabāh	بلال بن رَبَاح
Hamzah bin ‘Abdul-Muttalib	حَمْزَة بن عبدالمطلب
Hātib bin Abū Balta‘ah	حاطِبْ بن ابي بلتعه
Hilāl bin Abū Khaulā	هِلَال بن ابي خَولي
Iyās bin Bukair	اِيَاسْ بن بُكَيْر
‘Iyād bin Zuhair Al-Fihrī	عِيَاض بن زهيرالفهري
Kathīr bin ‘Amr As-Salamī	كَثِير بن عمروالسَّلمي
Khunais bin Hudhāfah	خُنَيْس بن حذافة
Mālik bin ‘Amr As-Salamī	مَالِكْ بن عمروالسلمي
Mālik bin Abū Khaulā Al-Ju‘fī	مَالِكْ بن ابي خولي الجُعفي
Mālik bin ‘Umailah	مَالِكْ بن عُمَيله
Mālik bin Umayyah bin ‘Amr As-Salamī	مَالِك بن اميه بن عمرو السلمي
Ma‘mar bin Abū As-Sarh	مَعْمَرْ بن ابي السرح
Marthad bin Abū Marthad Al-Ghanawī	مَرْثَدْبن ابي مرثد الغنوي
Mas‘ūd bin Rabī‘ah Al-Qārī	مَسْعُود بن ربيعه القاري
Midlāj bin ’Amr Al-Aslamī	مِدْلَاج بن عمرو ا الأسلمي
Mihja‘ bin Sālih Al-Muhājir	مِهْجَعْ بن صالح المهاجر

Mu'attib bin Hamrā' Al-Khuzā'ī As-Salūlī	مُعَتِّبْ بن حمراء الخزاعي السلولي
Muhammad, The Messenger of Allah ﷺ	مُحَمَّد رسول اللّٰه
Muhriz bin Nadlah Al-'Asadī	مُحْرِز بن نَضْله الأسدي
Mus'ab bin 'Umair Al-'Abdarī	مُصْعَبْ بن عمير العَبْدري
Qudāmah bin Maz'ūn Al-Jumahī	قُدامَه بن مظعون الجمحي
Rabī'ah bin Aktham bin Sakhbarah Al-'Asadī	رَبيعَه بن اكثم بن سخبره الاَسدي
Sabrah bin Fātik Al-'Asadī	سَبره بن فاتك الاسدي
Sa'd bin Abū Waqqās	سَعْد بن ابي وقاص
Sa'd bin Khaulā	سَعْد بن خولي
Safwān bin Baidā' Al-Fihrī	صَفْوَان بن بيضاء الفهري
Sahl bin Baidā' Al-Fihrī	سَهل بن بيضاء الفِهري
Sā'ib bin 'Uthmān bin Maz'ūn	سَائِبْ بن عثمان بن مظعون
Sāib Maz'ūn Al-Jumahī	سَائِبْ بن مظعون الجمحي
Sa'īd bin Zaid bin 'Amr bin Nufail	سَعِيد بن زيد بن عمرو بن نفيل
Sālim bin M'aqal	سَالِمْ بن معقل
Salīt bin 'Amr Al-'Āmarī	سَلِيط بن عمرو العامري
Shammās bin 'Uthmān Al-Makhzūmī	شَمَّاس بن عثمان المخزومي

Shujā‘ bin Wahab or Abū Wahab Al-’Asadī	شُجَاع بن وهب يا ابي وهب الاسدي
Shuqrān Habashī	شُقْرَان حبشي
Suhaib bin Sinān Ar-Rūmī	صُهَيْب بن سنان الرومي
Suwaibit bin Harmalah	سَوَيْبِط بن حرملة
Suwaibit bin Sa‘d Al-Qurashī	سَوَيْبِط بن سعد القرشي
Suwaid bin Makhshī At-Tāi	سُوَيْد بن مَخْشِي الطائي
Talhah bin ‘Ubaidullāh At-Taimī	طَلْحه بن عبيدالله التيمي
Tufail bin Al-Hārith Al-Muttalabī	طُفَيْل بن الحارث المطلبي
Tulaib bin ‘Umair	طُلَيْب بن عمير
‘Ubaidah bin Hārith Al-Qurashī	عُبَيْدَه بن حارث القرشي
‘Umair bin Abū Waqqās Az-Zuhrī	عُمَيْر بن ابي وقاص الزهري
‘Umair bin ‘Auf servant of Suhail Al-‘Āmirī	عُمَيْر بن عوف مولىٰ سهيل العامري
‘Umar bin Al-Khattāb Al-Fārūq	عُمَر بن الخطاب الفاروق
‘Uqbah bin Wahab	عُقْبَهْ بن وهب
‘Uthmān bin ‘Affān Dhū-Nūrain	عُثْمَان بن عَفَّان ذوالنوّرين
‘Uthmān bin Maz‘ūn Al-Jumahī	عُثْمَان بن مظعون الجمحي
Wahab bin Abū Sarh Al-Fihrī	وَهب بن ابي سرح الفهري
Wahab bin Mihsan Al-’Asadī	وَهب بن محصن الأسدي
Wahab bin Sa‘d bin Abū Sarh	وَهْبْ بن سعد بن ابي سرح

Wāqid bin ʻAbdullāh At-Tamīmī Al-Yarbuī	وَاقِدْ بن عبدالله التميمي اليربوعي
Yazīd bin Ruqaish bin Ri'āb	يَزِيْد بن رقيش بن رئاب
Zāhir bin Harām Al-'Ashja'ī	زَاهِر بن حرام الاَشجعي
Zaid bin Al-Khattāb bin Nufail Al-ʻAdawī	زَيْد بن الخطاب بن نفيل العدوي
Zayād bin Kaʻb bin ʻAmr Al-Juhanī	زَيَاد بن كعب بن عمروالجهني
Zubair bin Al-ʻAwwām	زُبَيْر بن العوّام

The Participants of the Battle of Badr from the Ansār (Helpers)

‘Abas bin ‘Āmir bin ‘Adī Al-’Ansārī	عَبَس بن عامربن عدي الأنصاري
‘Abbād bin Bishr bin Waqsh	عَبَّاد بن بشربن وقش
‘Abbād bin Qais Az-Zuraqī	عباد بن قيس الزُّرقي
‘Abdu Rabbih bin Haq As-Sā‘idī	عبدُربِّه بن حق الساعدي
‘Abdullāh bin ‘Abd Munāf Al-’Ansārī	عَبْدُاللّٰه بن عبد مناف الأنصاري
‘Abdullāh bin ‘Abdullāh bin Ubayy	عَبْدُاللّٰه بن عبداللّٰه بن أُبَيّ
‘Abdullāh bin ‘Abs Al-’Ansārī	عَبْدُاللّٰه بن عبس الأنصاري
‘Abdullāh bin Al-Jadd bin Qais Al-’Ansārī	عَبْدُاللّٰه بن الجد بن قيس الأنصاري
‘Abdullāh bin ‘Āmir Al-Balawī Al-’Ansārī	عَبْدُاللّٰه بن عامر البَلَوي الأنصاري
‘Abdullāh bin ‘Amr bin Harām Al-’Ansārī	عَبْدُاللّٰه بن عمروبن حرام الأنصاري

'Abdullāh bin Jubair bin Numān Al-'Ansārī	عَبْدُاللّٰه بن جبير بن نعمان الأنصاري
'Abdullāh bin Ka'b Al-Māzinī	عَبْدُاللّٰه بن كعب المازني
'Abdullāh bin Nu'mān bin Baldhamah	عَبْدُاللّٰه بن نعمان بن بَلْذَمه
'Abdullāh bin Qais Al-'Ansārī	عَبْدُاللّٰه بن قيس الأنصاري
'Abdullāh bin Qais bin Sakhr Al-Khazrajī	عَبْدُ اللّٰه بن قيس بن صَخْر الخزرجي
'Abdullāh bin Rabī' Al-Khazrajī	عَبْدُاللّٰه بن ربيع الخزرجي
'Abdullāh bin Rawāhah Al-'Ansārī	عَبْدُاللّٰه بن رواحه الأنصاري
'Abdullāh bin Sa'd Al-'Ansārī Al-'Ausī	عَبْدُاللّٰه بن سعدالأنصاري الأوسي
'Abdullāh bin Sahl Al-'Ansārī	عَبْدُاللّٰه بن سَهْل الأنصاري
'Abdullāh bin Salimah Al-'Ansārī Al-Balawī	عَبْدُاللّٰه بن سَلمه الأنصاري البَلَوي
'Abdullāh bin Tāriq Al-Balawī	عَبْدُاللّٰه بن طارق البَلَوي
'Abdullāh bin Tha'labah Al-Balawī	عَبْدُاللّٰه بن ثعلبه البلوي
'Abdullāh bin 'Umair bin 'Adī	عَبْدُاللّٰه بن عُمير بن عدي
'Abdullāh bin 'Urfutah Al-'Ansāri	عَبْدُاللّٰه بن عُرفطه الأنصاري
'Abdullāh bin Zaid Al-'Ansārī	عَبْدُاللّٰه بن زيدالأنصاري

'Abdur Rahmān bin 'Abdullāh Al-Balawī	عَبدُالرحمٰن بن عبدالله البَلَوي
'Abdur Rahmān bin Jabr Al-'Ansārî	عَبدُالرحمٰن بن جَبْرالأنصاري
'Abdur Rahmān bin Ka'b Al-Māzinî	عَبدُالرحمٰن بن كعب المازني
Abū Ad-Diyāh Al-'Ansāri Al-'Ausī	ابو الضِّياح الأنصاري الأوسي
Abū Fudālah Al-'Ansārī	ابو فضاله الأنصاري
Abū 'Īsā Al-Hārithī Al-'Ansārī	ابوعيسيٰ الحارثي الأنصاري
Abū Lubābah Rifā'ah bin 'Abdul Mundhir	ابو لُبابه رِفَاعَه بن عبدالمنذر
Abū Mulail Al-'Ansārī Ad-Dubī'ī	ابو مُلَيل الأنصاري الضبيعي
Abū Qatādah bin Rib'ī Al-'Ansārī	ابو قتاده بن رِبْعي الأنصاري
Abū Sirmah Al-'Ansārī Al-Māzanī	ابو صِرْمَه الأنصاري المازني
'Abudllāh bin Al-Humair Al-'Ashja 'ī	عَبْدُالله بن الحُمَير الأشجعي
'Adī bin Abū Az-Zaghbā' Al-Juhanī	عَدِي بن ابي الزَّغْباء الجهني
'Ā'idh bin Mā'is Al-'Ansārī	عَائِذ بن ماعص الأنصاري
'Āmir bin 'Abd 'Amr Al-'Ansārī	عَامِر بن عبد عمروالأنصاري

‘Āmir bin Mukhallad Al-’Ansari Al-Khazrajī	عَامِر بن مُخَلَّد الأنصاري الخزرجي
‘Āmir bin Salamah bin ‘Āmir Al-Ansārī Al-Balawī	عَامِر بن سلمه بن عامر الأنصاري البلوي
‘Āmir bin Thābit Al-’Ansārī	عَامِر بن ثابت الأنصاري
‘Āmir bin Umayyah	عَامِر بن أميه
‘Amr bin Al-Jamūh Al-’Ansārī	عَمْرو بن الجَمُوح الأنصاري
‘Amr bin ‘Auf Al-’Ansārī	عَمْرو بن عوف الأنصاري
‘Amr bin Ghaziyyah Al-’Ansārī	عَمْرو بن غَزِيّه الأنصاري
‘Amr bin Iyās Al-Yamanī	عَمْرو بن اياس اليمني
‘Amr bin Mu‘ādh bin Nu‘mān	عَمْرو بن معاذ بن نعمان
‘Amr bin Ma‘bad	عَمْرو بن معبد
‘Amr bin Qais Al-Khazrajī	عَمْرو بن قيس الخزرجي
‘Amr bin Tha‘labah bin Wahab	عَمْرو بن ثعلبه بن وهب
‘Amr bin ‘Uqbah bin Nayāz Al-’Ansārī	عَمْرو بن عقبه بن نياز الأنصاري
Anas bin Ma‘ādh bin Anas	اَنَسْ بن معاذ بن انس
Anas bin Mālik bin Nadr	اَنَسْ بن مالك بن نضر
Ānisah (servant of the Messenger of Allāh ﷺ)	آنِسه مولي رسول الله
‘Antarah (servant of Sulaim bin ‘Amr bin Hadīdah)	عَنْتَرَه مولي سُليم بن عمرو بن حديده

As'ad bin Yazīd bin Al-Fākih	اَسْعَد بن يزيد بن الفاكه
'Āsim bin Bukair Al-'Ansārī	عَاصِم بن بُكير الأنصاري
'Āsim bin Qais Al-'Ansārī	عَاصِم بن قيس الأ نصاري
'Āsim bin Thābit Al-'Ansārī	عَاصِم بن ثابت الأنصاري
'Atiyyah bin Nuwairah	عَطيَّه بن نُوَيره
'Auf bin 'Afrā' Al-'Ansārī	عَوْف بن عَفراء الأنصاري
Aus bin Khawalī bin 'Abdullāh	اَوْس بن خَوَلي بن عبدالله
Aus bin Sāmit Al-'Ansārī	اَوْس بن صامت الأنصاري
Aus bin Thābit Al-'Ansārī	اَوْس بن ثابت الأنصاري
Bashīr bin Sa'd bin Tha'labah	بَشِيْر بن سعد بن ثعلبه
Bishr bin Brā' bin Ma'rūr	بِشْر بن براء بن معرور
Dahhāk bin 'Abd 'Amr Al-'Ansārī	ضَحّاك بن عبد عمروالأنصاري
Dahhāk bin Hārithah Al-Kharaji	ضحّاك بن حارثه الخزرجي
Fākih bin Bishr Al-'Ansārī Az-Zuraqī	فَاكه بن بشر الأنصاري الزرقي
Farwah bin 'Amr Al-'Ansārī	فَرْوَهْ بن عمروالأنصاري
Ghannām bin Aus bin Ghannām Al-'Ansārī	غنّام بن اوس بن غنّام الأنصاري
Hammām bin Hārith bin Damurah	همام بن حارث بن ضمره
Hamzah bin 'Amr Al-'Ansārī	حمزه بن عمرو الأنصاري

Hānī bin Niyār Al-Balawī	هاني بن نِيَارالبَلَوي
Hārithah bin Surāqah Al-'Ansārī An-Najjārī	حارِثه بن سُرَاقه الأنصاري النجاري
Hilāl bin Umayyah Al-'Ansārī Al-Wāqifī	هلال بن اميّه الأنصاري الواقفي
Hilāl bin Mu'allā Al-'Ansārī Al-Khazrajī	هلال بن معلىٰ الأنصاري الخزرجي
Hubail bin Wabrah Al-'Ansārī	هبيل بن وَبْره الأنصاري
'Ismah bin Al-Husain bin Wabrah	عِصْمَه بن الحُصين بن وبرة
'Ismah or 'Usaimah Al-'Asadī	عِصمه يا عُصيمة الأسدي
'Ismah or 'Usaimah Al-'Ashja'ī	عِصْمَه يا عُصيمه الأ شجعي
'Itbān bin Mālik Al-'Ansārī As-Sālimī	عِتْبَان بن مالك الأنصاري السالمي
Iyās bin Wadaqah Al-Khazrajī	اِيَاس بن ودَقَه الخزرجي
Jābir bin 'Abdullāh bin Ri'āb	جَابِر بن عبدالله بن رئاب
Jābir bin 'Atīk bin Qais Al-'Ausi	جَابِرْ بن عَتِيك بن قيس الأوسي
Ka'b bin 'Amr bin 'Abbād	كَعْب بن عمروبن عَبّاد
Ka'b bin Jammāz Al-'Ansārī	كَعْب بن جَمَّاز الأنصاري
Ka'b bin Zaid Al-'Ansārī	كَعْب بن زيد الأنصاري
Khalīfah bin 'Adī	خَلِيفَه بن عدي
Khallād bin Rāfi' bin Mālik Al-Khazrajī	خَلّاد بن رافع بن مالك الخزرجي

Khubaib bin 'Adi Al-'Ausī	خُبَيْب بن عدي الأوسي
Mu'ādh bin Jabal	مُعاذ بن جبل
Ma'bad bin 'Abbād Al-'Ansārī	مَعْبَد بن عباد الأنصاري
Ma'bad bin Qais bin Sakhr	مَعْبَد بن قيس بن صخر
Ma'bad bin Wahab Al-'Abdī	مَعْبَد بن وهب العبدي
Mālik bin Ad-Dukhshum Al-'Ansārī	مَالِك بن الدُخْشم الأنصاري
Mālik bin At-Tayyihān	مَالِك بن التيهان
Mālik bin Mas'ūd As-Sā'idī	مَالِك بن مسعود الساعدي
Mālik bin Numailah Al-Muzani	مَالِك بن نُميله المزني
Mālik bin Qudāmah Al-'Ansārī	مَالِك بن قُدامه الأنصاري
Mālik bin Rabī'ah Al-'Ansārī	مَالِك بن ربيعه الأنصاري
Mālik bin Rāfi' Az-Zuraqī	مَالِك بن رافع الزرقي
Ma'mar bin Harith Al-Qurashi	مَعْمَر بن حارث القرشي
Ma'n bin 'Adī Al-Balawī	مَعْن بن عدي البَلَوي
Ma'n bin 'Afrā Al-'Ansārī	معن بن عفراء الأنصاري
Ma'n bin Yazīd bin 'Akhnas As-Sulamī	مَعن بن يزيد بن اَخنس السُلمي
Ma'qil bin Al-Mundhir As-Sulamī	مَعْقِل بن المنذر السلمي
Mas'ūd bin 'Abd Mas'ūd Al-'Ausī	مَسْعُود بن عبد مسعود الأوسي

Mas'ūd bin Aus	مَسْعُود بن اَوس
Mas'ūd bin Khālid Az-Zuraqī	مَسْعُوْد بن خالد الزرقي
Mas'ūd bin Rabī'ah Al-Qārī	مَسْعُود بن ربيعه القاري
Mas'ūd bin Sa'd Az-Zuraqī	مَسْعُوْد بن سعدالزرقي
Mu'ādh bin Afrā' Al-'Ansārī	مُعَاذ بن عفراء الأنصاري
Mu'ādh bin 'Amr bin Jamūh	مُعَاذ بن عمروبن جموح
Mu'ādh bin Mā'is Al-'Ansārī	مُعَاذ بن مَاعِص الأنصاري
Mu'attib bin Qushair	مُعَتِّب بن قشير
Mu'attib bin 'Ubaid Al-Balawī	مُعَتِّب بن عبيد البلوي
Mu'awwidh bin 'Afrā'	مُعَوِّذ بن عفراء
Mubashshir bin 'Abdul Mundhir Al-'Ausī	مُبَشِّر بن عبدالمُنذر الأوسي
Muhammad bin Maslamah Al-'Ansārī	محمد بن مَسْلَمه الأنصاري
Muhraz bin 'Āmir	مُحْرَز بن عامر
Mujadhdhar bin Ziyād Al-Balwī Al-'Ansārī	مُجذَّربن ذِياد البَلَوي الأنصاري
Mulail bin Wabarah	مُلَيل بن وَبَره
Mundhir bin 'Arfajah Al-'Ausi Al-'Ansārī	مُنْذربن عَرْفَجه الأوسي الأنصاري
Mundhir bin Muhammad Al-'Ausī	مُنْذِربن محمّد الأوسي

Mundhir bin Qudāmah Al-'Ansārī Al-'Ausī	مُنذِر بن قدامه الأنصاري الأوسي
Murārah bin Rabī' Al-'Amrī	مُراره بن ربيع العَمْري
Nahhāt bin Tha'labah Al-Balawī	نَحّات بن ثَعْلَبَه البَلَوي
Nasr bin Hārith Al-'Ausi	نصربن حارث الأوسي
Naufal bin Tha'labah Al-'Ansārī	نَوْفل بن ثعلبه الأنصاري
Nu'aimān bin 'Amr bin Rifā'ah Al-'Ansārī	نُعَيْمان بن عمروبن رفاعه الأنصاري
Nu'mān bin 'Abd 'Amr An-Najjārī Al-'Ansārī	نعمان بن عبد عمرو النجاري الأنصاري
Nu'mān bin 'Amr bin Rifā'ah Al-'Ansārī	نعمان بن عمرو بن رفاعه الأنصاري
Nu'mān bin A'qar	نعمان بن اعقر
Nu'mān bin Mālik bin Tha'labah Al-'Ansārī	نعمان بن مالك ثعلبه الأنصاري
Nu'mān bin Qauqal	نعمان بن قوقل
Nu'mān bin Sinān Al-'Ansārī	نعمان بن سنان الأنصاري
Nu'mān bin Abū Khadhamah Al-'Ansārī	نعمان بن ابي خَذَمه الأنصاري
Qais bin Abū Sa'Sa'ah Al-Māzanī	قَيس بن ابو صعصعه المازني
Qais bin 'Amr bin Sahl	قَيْس بن عمرو بن سهل
Qais bin As-Sakan Al-Khazrajī	قَيس بن السكن الخزرجي

Qais bin Makhlad Al-'Ansārī Al-Māzanī	قَيْس بن مخلد الأنصاري المازني
Qais bin Mihsan Az-Zuraqī	قَيْس بن محصن الزرقي
Qatādah bin Nu'mān Az-Zufarī	قَتَادَه بن نعمان الظفري
Qatbah bin 'Āmir Al-Khazrajī	قَطْبَه بن عامرالخزرجي
Rifā'ah bin 'Amr Al-Juhāni	رِفَاعَه بن عمرو الجهاني
Rifā'ah bin 'Amr bin Zaid Al-Khazrajī	رِفَاعَه بن عمرو بن زيد الَخزرَجي
Rifā'ah bin Hārith bin Rifā'ah Al-'Ansārī	رِفَاعَه بن حارث بن رِفَاعَه الأنصاري
Rifā'ah bin Rāfi' bin Mālik	رِفَاعَه بن رافع بن مالك
Rubai' bin Iyās Al-'Ansārī	رُبَيْع بن إِياس الأنصاري
Sa'd bin Ar-Rabī' bin 'Amr	سَعْد بن الربيع بن عمرو
Sa'd bin Khaithamah Al-'Ausi	سَعْد بن خيثمه الأوسي
Sa'd bin Khaulā Al-Kalbī	سَعْد بن خولىٰ الكلبي
Sa'd bin Mu'ādh, Chief of Al-'Aus Tribe	سَعْد بن معاذ سيّد الأوس
Sa'd bin Sahl	سَعْد بن سهل
Sa'd bin 'Ubaid Al-'Ansārī Al-'Ausī	سَعْد بن عبيد الأنصاري الأوسي
Sa'd bin 'Uthmān bin Khaldah	سَعْد بن عثمان بن خَلْدة
Sa'd bin Zaid Zuraqī	سَعْد بن زيد زرقي

Sa'd, servant of 'Utbah bin Ghazwān	سَعْد موليٰ عتبه بن غَزْوان
Sahl bin 'Atīk Al-'Ansārī	سَهْل بن عتيك الأنصاري
Sahl bin Hunaif Al-'Ansārī Al-'Ausi	سَهْل بن حُنيف الأنصاري الأوسي
Sahl bin Qais Al-'Ansārī As-Sulami	سَهْل بن قيس الأنصاري السلمي
Sa'īd bin Suahil Al-'Ansārī Al-'Ashhalī	سَعيد بن سهيل الأنصاري الأشهلي
Salamah bin Hātib Al-'Ansārī	سَلَمه بن حاطب الأنصاري
Salamah bin Salāmah bin Waqsh	سَلَمه بن سلامة بن وقش
Salamah bin Thābit bin Waqsh	سَلَمه بن ثابت بن وَقْش
Sālim bin 'Umair Al-'Ansārī	سالِم بن عمير الأنصاري
Salīt bin Qais Al-'Ansārī	سَلِيط بن قيس الأنصاري
Salmah bin Aslam Al-'Ansārī Al-Hārithi	سَلَمه بن اسلم الأنصاري الحارثي
Sawād bin Ghaziyyah Al-'Ansārī	سَواد بن غَزيّة الأنصاري
Simāk bin Kharashah Al-'Ansārī	سِماك بن خَرَشه الأنصاري
Simāk bin Sa'd Al-'Ansārī	سِمَاك بن سعد الأنصاري
Sinān bin Abū Sinān	سِنان بن ابي سِنَان
Sinān bin Saifi	سِنَان بن صيفي
Sulaim bin 'Amr Al-'Ansārī As-Sulamī	سُلَيْم بن عمروالأنصاري السُلمي

Subai‘ bin Qais Al-Khazrajī	سُبَيْع بن قيس الخزرجي
Sufyān bin Bishr	سُفْيَان بن بشر
Sufyān bin Bishr Al-Khazrajī	سُفْيَان بن بشر الخزرجي
Suhail bin ‘Amr	سُهَيْل بن عمرو
Suhail bin Rāfi‘ Al-’Ansārī	سُهَيْل بن رافع الأنصاري
Sulaim bin Hārith Al-’Ansārī	سُلَيْم بن حارث الأنصاري
Sulaim bin Milhān Al-’Ansārī	سُلَيْم بن مِلحان الأنصاري
Sulaim bin Qais bin Qahad	سُلَيْم بن قيس بن قهد
Surāqah bin ‘Amr bin ‘Atiyyah Al-Khazrajī	سُرَاقَه بن عمرو بن عطيه الخزرجي
Surāqah bin Ka‘b bin ‘Amr	سُرَاقَه بن كعب بن عمرو
Swād bin Zaid Al-’Ansārī Al-Khazrajī	سَوَاد بن زيد الأنصاري الخزرجي
Thābit bin Akhram	ثَابت بن اخرم
Thābit bin ‘Amr bin Zaid Al-’Ansārī	ثَابت بن عمرو بن زيد الأَنصاري
Thābit bin ‘Amr bin Zaid bin ‘Adī	ثَابت بن عمرو بن زيد بن عدي
Thābit bin Hudhail	ثَابت بن هذيل
Thābit bin Jidha‘	ثَابِتْ بن جِذع
Thābit bin Khālid bin Nu‘mān Al-’Ansārī	ثَابت بن خالد بن نعمان الأَنصاري
Thābit bin ‘Ubaid Al-’Ansārī	ثَابت بن عبيدالأنصاري

Tha'labah bin 'Amr bin Mihsan	ثَعْلَبَه بن عمرو بن محصن
Tha'labah bin 'Anamah bin 'Adī	ثَعْلَبَه بن عَنَمة بن عدي
Tha'labah bin Hātib bin 'Amr	ثَعْلَبَه بن حاطب بن عمرو
Tufail bin Mālik Al-'Ansārī	طُفَيل بن مالك الأنصاري
'Ubād bin Qais Al-'Ansārī Al-Khazrajī	عُباد بن قيس الأنصاري الخزرجي
'Ubād bin 'Ubaid bin At-Tayyihān	عُباد بن عبيد بن التيِّهان
'Ubadah bin Al-Khashkhāsh	عُبادَه بن الخشخاش
'Ubādah bin Qais Al-'Ansārī	عُبادَه بن قيس الانصاري
'Ubādah bin Sāmit Al-'Ansārī	عُبادَه بن صامت الأنصاري
'Ubaid bin Abū 'Ubaid Al-'Ansārī	عُبَيْد بن ابوعبيدالأنصاري
'Ubaid bin Aus Al-'Ansārī	عُبَيْد بن اوس الأنصاري
'Ubaid bin Tayyihān Al-'Ansārī	عُبَيْد بن تيِّهان الأنصاري
'Ubaid bin Zaid bin 'Āmir Az-Zuraqī	عُبَيْد بن زيد بن عامر الزرقي
Ubayy bin Thābit Al-'Ansārī	اُبيّ بن ثابت الأنصاري
Ubayy bin Ka'b	اُبيّ بن كعب
'Umair bin Al-Humām	عُمَيْر بن الْحُمَام
'Umair bin 'Āmir Al-Khazrajī	عُمَيْر بن عامرالخزرجي
'Umair bin Harām bin 'Amr bin Jamūh	عُمَيْر بن حرام بن عمرو بن جموح

‘Umair bin Hārith bin Tha‘labah Al-’Ansārī	عُمَيْر بن حارث بن ثعلبه الأنصاري
‘Umair bin Ma‘bad bin Al-’Az‘ar	عُمَيْر بن معبد بن الأزعر
‘Umair bin Nayār Al-’Ansārī	عُمَيْر بن نيار الأنصاري
‘Umārah bin Hazm Al-’Ansārī	عُمَاره بن حزم الأنصاري
‘Umārah bin Zayād bin As-Sakan	عُمَاره بن زياد بن السكن
Unais bin Qatādah bin Rabī‘ah	أنَيْس بن قتادة بن ربيعه
‘Uqbah bin ‘Amr Al-’Ansārī	عُقْبَه بن عمروالأنصاري
‘Uqbah bin Rabī‘ah Al-’Ansārī	عُقْبَه بن ربيعه الأنصاري
‘Uqbah bin ‘Uthmān Al-’Ansārī	عُقْبَه بن عثمان الأنصاري
‘Uqbah bin Wahab bin Kaldah	عُقْبَه بن وهب بن كلده
‘Uqbah bin ‘Āmir bin Nābī Al-’Ansārī	عُقْبَه بن عامربن نابي الأنصاري
Usaid bin Hudair bin Simāk	أسيد بن حُضَير بن سِمَاك
Usaimah Al-Ashja‘ī	عُصَيْمَه الأشجعي
’Usair bin ‘Amr Al-’Ansārī	اُسَيْر بن عمروالأنصاري
‘Utbah bin ‘Abdullāh bin Sakhr	عُتْبَه بن عبدالله بن صخر
‘Utbah bin Ghazawān	عُتْبَه بن غزوان
‘Utbah bin Rabī‘ah Al-Baharāni Al-’Azdī	عُتْبَه بن ربيعه البهراني الأزدي
‘Uwaim bin Sā‘idah bin ‘Ā’ish	عُوَيْم بن ساعده بن عائش

‘Uwaimir bin Ashqar	عُوَيمر بن اشقر
Wadī‘ah bin ‘Amr Al-Juhanī	وديعه بن عمروالجهني
Wadqah or Wadfah bin Iyās Al-'Ansārī	وَدْقَه يا وَدْفه بن اِياس الأنصاري
Yazīd bin Akhnas As-Sulamī	يزيد بن اخنس السلمي
Yazīd bin ‘Āmir bin Hadīdah Al-Khazrajī	يزيد بن عامر بن حديدة الخزرجي
Yazīd bin Hārith Al-'Ansārī	يزيد بن حارث الأنصاري
Yazīd bin Mundhir Al-'Ansārī As-Sulamī	يزيد بن منذر الأنصاري السلمي
Yazīd bin Thābit Al-'Ansārī	يزيد بن ثابت الأنصاري
Yazīd bin Tha‘labah Khazamah	يزيد بن ثعلبه خَزَمه
Zaid bin Ad-Dathinah Al-Biyadī	زَيْد بن الدَثِنه البياضي
Zaid bin ‘Āsim Al-Māzanī Al-'Ansārī	زَيْد بن عاصم المازني الأنصاري
Zaid bin Aslam bin Tha‘labah Al-‘Ajlānī	زَيْد بن اسلم بن ثعلبه العجلاني
Zaid bin Muzuyun Al-'Ansārī	زَيْد بن المْزُين الأنصاري
Zaid bin Sahl Al-'Ansārī	زَيْد بن سهل الأنصاري
Zaid bin Wadī‘ah bin ‘Amr	زَيْد بن وديعه بن عمرو
Zayād bin Labīd Al-Bayādī	زَياد بن لبيد البياضي

The Commander Companions ﵃ of the Prophet ﷺ

‘Abdullāh bin Hudhāfah	عَبْدُ اللّٰه بن حُذافه
‘Abdullāh bin Jahash	عَبْدُاللّٰه بن جحش
‘Abdullāh bin Rawāhah	عَبْدُاللّٰه بن رَواحه
‘Abdur Rahmān bin ‘Auf	عَبْدُالرَّحْمٰن بن عوف
Abu ‘Ubaidah bin Al-Jarrāh	ابو عُبَيْدَه ابن الجرّاح
Amr bin Al-‘Ās	عَمْرُو بن العاص
‘Āsim bin Thābit	عَاصِمْ بن ثابت
Darrār bin Azwar Asadi	ضِرّار بن ازور اسدي
Hudhaifah bin Yamān	حُذَيْفَه بن يمان
‘Ikrimah bin Abū Hishām	عِكْرِمَه بن ابي هشام
Ja‘far bin Abū Tālib	جَعْفَرْ بن ابي طالب
Jarīr bin ‘Abdullāh bin Jābir	جَرِيْر بن عبداللّٰه بن جابر
Khālid bin Walīd	خَالِد بن وليد
Muthannā bin Hārithah	مُثَنّٰى بن حارثه
Nu‘mān bin Muqarrin	نُعْمَان بن مقرّن

Qa'qa' bin 'Amr	قَعْقَاع بن عمرو
Sa'd bin Abū Waqqās	سَعْد بن ابي وقاص
Sa'īd bin Al-'Ās	سَعِيْد بن العاص
Salmah bin Qais	سَلمَه بن قيس
Shurahbīl bin Hasanah	شُرَحبِيل بن حَسَنَه
'Ubādah bin As-Sāmit	عُبادَة بن الصّامت
'Ukāshah bin Mihsan	عُكاشَه بن مِحْصن
'Usāmah bin Sa'īd	اُسامه بن سعيد
'Utbah bin Ghazawān	عُتْبَه بن غزوان
Zaid bin Hārithah	زَيْد بن حارثه

The Eminent Female Companions رضي الله عنهن of the Messenger of Allah ﷺ

Asmā' bint 'Umais bint Ma'd	اسماء بنت عُميس بن مَعْد
Asmā' bint Yazīd	اَسْمَاء بنت يزيد
Asmā' bint Abū Bakr As-Siddīq	اسماء بنت ابو بكر الصدّيق
Fātimah bint Al-Khattāb	فاطمة بنت الخطاب
Fātimah bint Asad	فَاطِمَة بنت اسد
Fātimah bint Qais bin Khālid	فاطمة بنت قيس بن خالد
Hamnah bint Jahsh	حَمْنَه بنت جحش
Hind bint 'Utbah	هِند بنت عتبه
Khansā' bint 'Amr Tamādir	خَنْسَاء بنت عمرو تماضر
Khaulah bint Hakīm	خَوْلَه بنت حكيم
Rubayyi' bint Mu'āwwidh bin 'Afrā'	رُبيّع بنت معوذ بن عفراء
Safiyyah bint 'Abdul Muttalib	صَفِيّه بنت عبدالمطلب
Shifā' bint 'Abdullāh	شِفَاء بنت عبداللّٰه
Sumayyah bint Khabbāt	سُمَيَّه بنت خبّاط
Umāmah bint Abū Al-'Ās	اُمَامَه بنت ابي العاص
Umm Abū Hurairah, Umaimah bint Subaih or Sufaih bint Al-Harith	ام ابي هريره، اميمه بنت صبيح يا صفيح بنت الحارث

Umm Aimen Barkat bint Tha'labah	ام اَيْمَنْ برکت بنت ثعلبه
Umm 'Ammārah Nasībah bint Ka'b	ام عماره نَسِيْبَه بنت كعب
Umm 'Atiyyah Nasībah bint Al-Hārith	ام عطيه نسيبه بنت الحارث
Umm Hakīm bint Zubair	ام حكيم بنت زبير
Umm Hānī Fākhtah bint Abū Tālib	ام هاني فاخته بنت ابي طالب
Umm Harām bint Milhān	ام حرام بنت ملحان
Umm Kulthūm bint 'Aqabah	ام كُلثُوم بنت عقبه
Umm Rūmān bint 'Āmir bin 'Uwaimir	ام رُوْمَان بنت عامر بن عُويمر
Umm Sulaim Sahlah bint Milhān	ام سُلَيْم سَهْلَة بنت ملحان
Umm Al-Fadl Lubābah bint Al-Hārith	ام الفضل لُبَابَهْ بنت الحارث
Umm Warqah bint 'Abdullāh	ام وَرْقَهْ بنت عبدالله
Zainab bint Abū Mu'āwiyah	زينب بنت ابى معاويه
Zainab bint Abū Salimah	زَيْنَب بنت ابى سلمه

The Female Companions ﵅ Who Learned the Qur'ān by Heart

'Ā'ishah Siddīqah	عائشه صديقه
Hafsah	حفصه
Umm Salamah	ام سلمه
Umm Warqah	سيده ام ورقه

The Female Companions ﵅ Who Learned a Portion of the Qur'ān

Hind bint 'Usaid	هند بنت اُسَيد
Rā'itah bint Hayyān	رائطه بنت حيّان
Umm Hishām bint Hārithah	ام هشام بنت حارثه
Umm Sa'd bint Sa'd bin Ar-Rabī'	ام سعد بنت سعد بن الربيع

The Exegete amongst the Female Companions ﵅

'Ā'ishah Siddīqah	عائشه صديقه

The Traditionists amongst the Female Companions رضي الله عنهن of the Prophet ﷺ

'Ā'ishah Siddīqah	عائشه صديقه
Asmā' bint Abū Bakr	اسماء بنت ابى بكر
Fātimah bint Qais	فاطمة بنت قيس
Umm 'Atiyyah Al-'Ansārīyah	ام عطيه الأنصاريه
Umm Hānī Al-'Ansārīyah	ام هانى الأنصاريه
Umm Salamah	ام سلمه

The Female Jurist and Scholar Companions رضي الله عنهن

'Ā'ishah Siddīqah	عائشه صديقه
Asmā' bint Abū Bakr	اسماء بنت ابي بكر
'Ātikah bint Zaid	عَاتِكَهْ بنت زيد
Fātimah Az-Zahrā'	فاطمة الزهراء
Fātimah bint Qais	فاطمة بنت قيس
Hafsah bint 'Umar	حفصه بنت عمر
Haulā' bint Tuwait	حَولَاء بنت تُوَيت
Juwairiyyah	جويريه

Lailā bint Qānif	ليلیٰ بنت قانِف
Maimūnah	ميمونه
Safiyyah	صَفِيّه
Sahlah bint Suhail	سَهله بنت سهيل
Umm Ad-Dardā' Khairah bint Abū Hadrad Al-'Aslamī	ام الدَرداء خَيرة بنت ابي حَدْرد الأسلمي
Umm 'Aiman	ام ايمن
Umm 'Atiyyah	ام عطيه
Umm Habībah	ام حبيبه
Umm Salamah	ام سلمه
Umm Sharīk	ام شريك
Zainab bint Abū Salamah	زينب بنت ابى سَلَمه

The Expert in Heritage amongst the Female Companions رضي الله عنهن

'Ā'ishah Siddīqah	عائشه صديقه

The Expert Female Companion رضي الله عنها in the Secrets of the Sharīaḥ

Umm Salamah	ام سلمه

The Orator Female Companion ﷺ

Asmā' bint Yazīd bin Sakan	اسماء بنت یزید بن سکن

The Interpreter of Dreams

Asmā' bint 'Umais bin Ma'd	اسماء بنت عمیس بن مَعد

The Expert Female Companions ﷺ in the Science of Medicine and Surgery

Hamnah bint Jahsh	حَمْنَه بنت جَحش
Lailā Al-Ghifāriyah	لیلیٰ الغفاریه
Mu'ādhah Al-Ghifāriyah	معاذه الغِفاریة
Rubayyi' bint Mu'awwidh	رُبَیِّع بنت مُعَوِّذ
Rufaidah Aslamiyyah (she had a hospital)	رفیده اسلمیه
Umaimah bint Qais	اُمَیْمَه بنت قیس
Umm Atiyyah	ام عطیه
Umm Kabashah Al-Qudā'iyyah	ام کبشه القُضَاعیة
Umm Muta Al-Aslamiyah	ام مُطاع الأسلمیه
Umm Sulaim	ام سلیم

Umm Zayād Al-'Ashja'iyyah	ام زياد الأشجعية

The Eminent Poetess amongst the Female Companions رضي الله عنهن

'Ātikah bint Zaid	عاتكه بنت زيد
Hind bint Hārith	هند بنت حارث
Hind bint Uthāthah	هند بنت اثاثه
Kabasha bint Rāfi'	كبشه بنت رافع
Khansa' bint 'Amr	خنساء بنت عمرو
Maimūnah bint 'Abdullāh Balawiyyah	ميمونه بنت عبدالله بلويه
Nu'm, wife of Shammās	نُعْم امراة شمّاس
Qatīlah bint An-Nadr Al-'Abdariyyah	قتيله بنت النضر العبدريه
Ruqayyah	رقيه
Sa'dā bint Kurz	سعدىٰ بنت كرز
Safiyyah bint Abdul Muttalib	صَفِيّه بنت عبدالمطلب
Umāmah Al-Mazīdiyyah	امامه المَزِيدِيّه
Umm Aiman	ام ايمن
Zainab bint 'Awwām	زينب بنت عوّام

The Scribes amongst the Female Companions ﵅ of the Prophet ﷺ

Hafsah bint 'Umar bin Al-Khattāb	حفصه بنت عمر بن الخطاب
Shifā bint 'Abdullāh	شفاء بنت عبدالله
Umm Kulthūm bint 'Aqabah	ام كلثوم عقبه

The Traders amongst the Female Companions ﵅ of the Prophet ﷺ

Asmā' bint Mukharribah	اسماء بنت مُخَرِّبه
Haulā' bint Tuwait	حولاء بنت تويت
Khadījah Al-Kubrā	خديجة الكبرى
Malīkah Umm As-Sā'ib	مليكة ام السائب
Thaqafiyyah	ثقفيه

Chapter: 5

Qur'ānic Names for the Muslim Males and Females

- The Blessed Names taken from the Noble Qur'ān
- The Qur'ānic Names according to the Roots of the Words
- The Qur'ānic Names as their Derivatives

Qur'ānic Names for the Muslim Males

Abān (اَبَان) Clear, manifest

'Abbād (عَبَّاد) Worshiper, servant, adorer

'Abbās (عَبَّاس) Very stern and austere, lion

'Ābid (عَابِد) Worshiper, adorer, servant

'Abīr (عَبِير)A wayfarer, perfume composed of various aromatics, numerous

'Abdān (عَبْدَان) Worshiper

'Ābis (عَابِس) Austere, stern, lion

Abrār (اَبْرَار) Pious, benevolent, philanthropist

Absār (اَبْصَار) Eyes, sagacious, discerning

Adhīn (اَذِين) Guarantor, chief, leader

Ādhin (آذِن) One who permits, allows, watcher, attendant

'Ādil (عَادِل) Just, fair, equitable, unbiased

'Adīl (عَدِيْل) Equal in weight or measure, like, parallel, brother in law

'Adnān (عَدْنَان) Everlasting, eternal, unchanging

Āfāq (آفَاقْ) Horizon, distant regions or lands

'Affān (عَفَّان) Very merciful, forgiving

Aflah (اَفْلَح) Most successful, prosperous

Afrah (اَفْرَه) Clever, gifted, having bright face

Ahad (اَحَد) Alone, unique

'Ahīd (عَهِيد) A confederate,

bound by a covenant, old

Ahmad (اَحْمَد) Eulogist, most praiser

Ahmar (اَحْمَر) Red

Ahsan (اَحْسَن) The best

'Ā'idh (عَائِذ) Seeking shelter, wanting protection

'Ajlān (عَجْلَان) Hasty, speedy, quick

Ajmal (اَجْمَل) Most beautiful, handsome

Ajwād (اَجْوَاد) Generous, bountiful, munificent, sagacious

Akhlāq (اَخْلَاق) Moral, ethics, manners

'Ākif (عَاكِف) Devoted to, preserving in, keeping to

Akīl (اَكِيل) Chum friend, boon companion, great eater

Akram (اَكْرَم) Most honorable, exalted, illustrious

'Alā' (عَلَاء) Highness, sublimity, dignity, superiority

Albāb (اَلْبَاب) Intellectual, wise

'Alī (عَلِي) High, elevated, lofty, eminent

Altāf (اَلْطَاف) Gentleness, benevolence

Amānat (اَمَانت) Trustworthiness, faithfulness, one who confides in everyone

Amīm (اَمِيم) Tall statured, high

Amīn (اَمِين) Trusted, honest, confided in

Amīr (اَمِير) Chief, leader, lord

Amjad (اَمْجَد) Glorified, illustrious, more noble

'Ammār (عَمَّار) To populate, make inhabited

'Amr (عَمْرو) Population, inhabited

Amthal (اَمْثَل) Optimum, ideal, model

Anīl (اَنِيْل) To get, obtain, attain, achieve

Anīs (اَنِيْس) Intimate friend, socialable, tamed

Ansar (اَنْصَر) Helpful, supportive

Anwar (اَنْوَرْ) Illuminated, radiant, bright

Anwār (اَنْوَار) Lights

Anzar (اَنْظَر) Observer, guardian, watcher

'Āqīb (عَاقِب) Coming after

'Aqīb (عَقِيْب) That which follows sequent, in order

'Aqīd (عَقِيد) Ally, confederate, bound, one who joins a contract

'Aqil (عَاقِل) Wise, sensible, intelligent, sagacious

'Aqīl (عَقِيْل) Wise, intelligent, sensible

Aqmar (اَقْمَر) Bright with moon light, dusky white dingy

Aqra' (اَقْرَع) Knocker, to draw near home, to give the best

Aqwas (اَقْوَس) Sharp, clever, experienced

Ārib (آرِبْ) Shrewd, sagacious, skilful

'Ārif (عَارِف) Knowing, familiar with, patient

'Arīf (عَرِيف) Chief inspector, overseer, monitor

Arqam (اَرْقَم) Writer, sign bearer

Arshad (اَرْشَد) Guide, directed

As'ad (اَسْعَد) Luckiest, happiest, helpr

Asghar (اَصْغَر) Smaller, junior, minimal

Ash'ar (اَشْعَر) Sensible, hairy, most knowing, poetical

Ashfāq (اَشْفَاق) Pity, compassions

Āshir (عَاشِر) Tenth, one who receives the tithes

'Asīb (عَصِيب) Critical, crucial, serious, difficult

'Āsil (عَاسِل) Beehive, a gatherer of honey, praised, quivering

'Āsim (عَاصِم) Protector, guardian, defender

'Asīm (عَصِيم) Defender, protector

Asjal (اَسْجَل) Wealthy, generous

Aslam (اَسْلَم) Immune, intact, flawless

Asrār (اَسْرَار) Secrets

'Assāl (عَسَّال) A gatherer of honey

'Assār (عَسَّار) Difficult, hard, indigent

Athīr (اَثِير) Noble, exalted, favorite

'Ātif (عَاطِف) Affectionate, kind, sympathetic

'Atīq (عَتِيق) Ancient, good, excellent, choice, generous

'Ātiq (عَاتِق) Shoulder, free

'Atiyyah (عَطِيَّه) Act of giving, gift, salary or wages

'Attāf (عَطَّاف) Affectionate, kind

'Atūf (عَطُوف) Affectionate, kind, pitiful, loving

Atyab (اَطْيَب) Perfumed, scented, pure, sacred

'Aun (عَوْن) Aid, help, assistance, aider, assistant

Ausāf (اَوْصَاف) Qualities, attributes

Ayās (اَيَاس) Hopeless, despaired

Ayyūb (اَيُّوب) One who returns frequently

Azhar (اَزْهَر) Radiant, shining moon

'Āzib (عَازِب) Distant, remote

'Āzim (عَازِم) Resolved to or on, determined to

'Azīm (عَزِيم) Firm, decided, resolute

'Azīm (عَظِيم) Great, immense, grand, important

Azraq (اَزْرَق) Blue

Badī' (بَدِيع) Splendid, astonishing, inventor, discoverer

Bahīj (بَهِيج) Delighted, happy, pleasant

Ba'īth (بَعِيث) Envoy, delegate

Bakīr (بَكِيرْ) New, earlier

Bākir (بَاكِر) Premature, early

Bakr (بَكْر) Early morning

Balīgh (بَلِيغ) Eloquent, well spoken, profound, serious

Barā' (بَرَاء) Innocent of, free from

Barkat (بَرْكَت) Blessing, prosperity, fortune

Bashārat (بَشَارَت) Good news, good omen

Bashīr (بَشِير) Bearer of good news, evangelist

Bāsiq (بَاسِق) Lofty, exceedingly white cloud, tall palm tree

Basīr (بَصِير) Discerning, shrewd, well informed

Bāsir (بَاصِر) Observer, one who sees, intelligent

Basīt (بَسِيط) Naive, simple, modest

Bāsit (بَاسِط) Who amplifies, enlarges, makes plentiful

Bishr (بِشْر) Joy

Budail (بُدَيْل) Reward, compensation, substitute

Buhairah (بُحَيْرَه) Lake, a small sea

Bukair (بُكَيْر) New, early, unprecedented

Burhān (بُرْهَان) Proof, evidence

Dābir (دَابِر) Root, origin, part, following

Dahhāk (ضَحَّاك) One who laughs much

Dāhik (ضَاحِك) Laughing, bright, happy

Dhakīr (ذَكِير) Having a good memory, more rememberer

Dā'im (دَائِم) Always, continuing, enduring, lasting

Dāmir (ضَامِر) Lean, thin

Damīr (ضَمِير) Conscience, heart, secret thought

Dāris (دَارِس) Illegible, one

who studies, a road much beaten by passengers

Darrāk (دَرَّاك) Intelligent, one who comprehends

Darrār (ضَرَّار) Most harming

Dāwūd (دَاود) Friend, companion

Dhabīh (ذَبِيْح) Cut, slaughtered, sacrificed

Dhahīb (ذَهِيب) Gilt, gild, having gilt lines

Dhahīl (ذَهِيل) Absent, to melt

Dhākir (ذَاكِر) Rememberer

Dhīshān (ذِيْشَان) Important, weighty, momentous

Dhuhaib (ذُهَيْب) A piece of gold

Dhulkifl (ذُوالْكِفْل) Guarantor, one who cares for

Dhul-Qarnaian (ذُوالقَرْنَيْن) Having two horns

Dhun-Nūn (ذُوالنُّوْن) Jonah (of the great fish), title of a Prophet عليه السلام

Dihāq (ضِحَاك) Full, abundant

Diyā' (ضِيَاء) Light, brightness, gleam

Dumair (ضُمَيْر) Secret, innermost

Dumām (ضُمَام) To join, a string, cord to draw and join a thing

Fadal (فَضَل) To remain over, exceed, excel, superflous

Fādil (فَاضِل) Superior, virtuous, generous

Fahīm (فَهِيم) Very intelligent, discerning, sagacious, judicious

Fā'id (فَائِض) Plentiful, superabundant, excess, copious

Faid (فَيْض) Abundance, flow, affluence, emanation

Faidān (فَيْضَان) Flood, plenty, great gift

Faisal (فَيْصَل) Judge, arbiter, sharp sword

Fā'iz (فَائِز) Successful, one

who escapes

Fākhir (فَاخِر) Excellent, superior, fancy, superb

Fakhr (فَخْر) Glory, excellence, pride, honor

Fākih (فَاكِه) Cheerful , merry, to jest with someone

Fālih (فَالِح) Successful, prosperous

Farah (فَرَح) Joy, gladness, festivity, happiness

Farhān (فَرْحَان) Glad, happy, cheerful

Farhat (فَرْحَت) Occasion of joy or gladness

Farīd (فَرِيد) Unique, matchless

Fārih (فَارِه) Skilful, brisk, active, lively

Fārūq (فَارُوق) Distinction of truth and error, fearing much

Fātih (فَاتِح) Opener, conqueror, indicator

Fātir (فَاطِر) Creator, originator, one who has eaten breakfast

Fayyād (فَيَّاض) Bountiful, munificent, overflowing (river)

Fu'ād (فُؤَاد) Heart, soul, mind

Fudail (فُضَيْل) Distinguished, excellent, noble

Furāt (فُرَات) Sweet water

Furqān (فُرْقَان)Test or distinction of truth and error, proof down

Ghaffār (غَفَّار) Merciful, forgiving, tolerant, ready to forgive

Ghāfir (غَافِر) Forgiving

Ghafūr (غَفُور) Merciful, forgiving, condoling

Ghālib (غَالِب) Victor, conqueror

Ghamām (غَمَام) Cloud, white clouds

Ghanī (غَنِي) Rich, in comfortable circumstances

Ghāzī (غَازِي) The participant in a Ghazwah, one who goes for a fight

Ghiyāth (غِيَاث) Aid, succor, an aider

Ghufrān (غُفْرَان) Pardon, forgiveness, remission, condonation

Habīb (حَبِيب) Sweetheart, beloved, lover

Habīt (هَبِيط) Emaciated, to descend

Hadhīr (حَذِير) One who gives cautions or warning

Hādhir (حَاذِر) Cautious, ready, beware

Hādī (هَادِي) Guide, leader, conductor, pilot

Hadīd (حَدِيد) Iron

Hafīz (حَفِيظ) Guardian, governor, watcher

Hājiz (حَاجِز) Barrier, partition, a just judge

Hakīm (حَكِيم) Wise, sage, judicious

Halīm (حَلِيم) Gentle, gracious, forgiving

Hamd (حَمْد) Praised, praiseworthy

Hamdān (حمدان) Praiser, a great praiser

Hamīd (حَمِيد) Praised, louded, commended

Hāmid (حَامِد)Praiser, thank giver

Hamīl (حَمِيل) Captive, foundling, stranger, guarantor

Hāmil (حَامِل) Pregnant, bearer, laden with fruit

Hamīr (حَمِير) Red skin

Hammād (حَمَّاد) One who praises most, a frequent praiser

Hamūd (حَمُود) Praised, eulogized, praiser

Hamūl (حَمُوْل) Patient, wise

Hanīf (حَنِيف) Sincere in religion, true, orthodox

Haqqānī (حقَّانِي) One who is genuine, justness, rightness

Harīj (حَرِيج) Narrow, tight, close

Harīm (حَرِيْم)Venerable, apartments of the women

Harīry (حَرِيري) Silk weaver, silk manufacturer

Harīth (حَرِيث) Ploughman

Harrār (حَرَّار) Silk trader, silk manufacturer

Hārūn (هَارُون) Name of a Prophetﷺ, chief, one who leads, strong

Hasan (حَسَن) Handsome, nice, pleasant

Hasanāt (حَسَنَات) Good deeds, benefits, alms

Hāshir (حَاشِر) Gatherer, assembler, collector

Hasīb (حَصِيب) One who throws stones

Hasīb (حَسِيب) Esteemed, avenger, sufficient

Hasīn (حَصِين) Well fortified, inaccessible, immune

Hasnain (حَسنين) Two beautiful (persons)

Hassān (حَسَّان) Very handsome, pretty, pious

Hātib (حَاطِب) Wood collector

Hilāl (هِلاَل) New moon, crescent, the first and last quarter of the moon

Hujjāj (حُجَّاج) The pilgrims to Makkah

Hussain (حُسَيْن) Good, handsome, a high mountain

I'jāz (اِعْجَاز) Eloquence, articulate, well spoken

'Abdān (عَبْدَان) Worshiper

Ibrāhīm (اِبْرَاهِيم) Servant, name of the exalted Prophetﷺ

Idrīs (اِدرِيْس) Knowledgeable, educationer, name of a Prophetﷺ

Ihsān (اِحْسَان) Kindness, benevolence, virtue

Ijlāl (اِجْلَال) Esteem, exaltation

Ikhlās (اِخْلَاص) Sincerity, consciousness, honest

Ikrām (اِكْرَام) Honor,

hospitality, tribute

'Imād (عِمَاد) Support, pillar, lofty building

'Imrān (عِمْرَان) Building, civilization, prosperity, populous

Imtinān (اِمْتِنَان) Gratitude, debtedness

Imtiyāz (اِمْتِيَاز) Distinction, characterized, excellence

In'ām (اِنْعَام) Gift, favor, boon

Indimām (اِنْضِمَام) Joining, entry, gathered, collected

'Irfān (عِرْفَان) Knowing, informed, learned

Irshād (اِرْشَاد) Guidance, counsel, advice

Irtadā (اِرْتَضِي) To be satisfied, pleased (with) consent (to)

'Isā (عيسيٰ) Life giver, protector from sins

'Isām (عِصَام) Strap, cord for tying a water skin, look

Ishāq (اِسْحَاق) Laughing, name of a Prophet عليه السلام

Isbāh (اِصْبَاح) Brighten, to come in the morning

Ishfāq (اِشْفَاق) Sympathy, compassions

Ishhād (اِشْهَاد) Witness, to make a witness, to testify

Isma'īl (اِسْمَاعِيل) O'Allāh! listen, happiness, brave, name of a Prophet عليه السلام

'Ismat (عِصْمَت) Prevention, defense, self restraint, sinlessness

'Itbān (عِتْبَان) Admonishment, friendly reproach, censure

Jalāl (جَلَال) Splendor, loftiness, power

Jālib (جَالِب) Importer, fetcher

Jalīl (جَلِيل) Great, sublime, glorious

Jalīs (جَلِيس) Companion, intimate friend

Jamāl (جَمَال) Beauty, elegance, graceful

Jamīl (جَمِيل) Handsome,

beautiful, fair, favor

Joudat (جَوْدَت) Goodness, excellence, partition, obstacle

Junaid (جُنَيْد) Pious, a small army

Ka'b (كَعْب) Heel, glory, honor, bottom, tail

Kādih (كَادِح) Toiling, industrious, laborious

Kafīl (كَفِيل) Guarantor, warrantor, sponsor

Kalīm (كَلِيم) Wounded, injured, speaker

Kamāl (كَمَال) Perfection, completeness, completion, integrity

Karāmat (كَرَامَت) Dignity, honor, respect, charisma, miracle

Karīm (كَرِيم) Generous, liberal, kind, hospitable, high born, noble

Karrār (كَرَّار) Repeater, reiterate, redoer, title of Ali رضي الله عنه

Kashshāf (كَشَّاف) One who reveals, discloses

Kāshif (كَاشِف) To reveal, to disclose, to inform about

Kāsib (كَاسِب) Winner, gainer

Kathīr (كَثِير) Much, many, numerous, abundant

Kāzim (كَاظِم) Repressor

Khabīr (خَبِيْر) Well informed, skilful, specialist.

Khadād (خَضَاد) A thornless plant, languor and pain

Khadīr (خَضِير) Green, verdant

Khairah (خَيْرَه) Good thing, good deed, choice

Khairūn (خَيْرُون) Better, good

Khalāq (خَلَاق) Portion, a good and just share, creator

Khalīd (خَلِيد) Eternal, durable, unalterable

Khālid (خَالِد) Eternal, ageless, unalterable

Khalīl (خَلِيْل) Friend, Intimate and sincere friend

Khalīq (خَلِيق) Fit, appropriate, perfect and complete

Khāliq (خَالِق) Creator, a worker

Khallād (خَلَّاد) Immortal, durable, unalterable

Khāmid (خَامِد) Silent, motionless, silent and dead

Khanīs (خَنِيس) To recede, one who remains behind

Khansān (خَنْسَان) One who hides oneself

Kibriyā (كِبْرِيَا) Pride, haughtiness, grandeur, glory

Kifāyat (كِفايَت) Sufficiency, adequacy, full supply

Kuraīb (كُرَيْب) Anguished, suffering one, grieved

Labīb (لَبِيب) Intelligent, rational, wise, sagacious, prudent

Lahīm (لَحِيم) Fat, plump

Lā'ib (لَاعِب) Player, athlete, sportsman, sport, gymnast

Latīf (لَطِيف) Gentle, soft, pleasant, delicate, thin

Luqmān (لُقْمَان) Wise, experienced

Lutf (لُطْف) Kindness, friendliness

Ma'n (مَعْن) The drawing of water, stream, beneficial

Ma'āb (مَآب) Retreat, resort, recourse, place to return to

Ma'ādh (مَعَاذ) Refuge, shelter, asylum, sanctuary

Ma'ārib (مَآرِب) Purpose, goals, aims

Madīd (مَدِيد) Long

Mahdī (مَهْدِي) Rightly guided, directed, showed the right way

Mahīs (مَحِيص) Strongly twisted

Mahmūd (مَحْمُود) Praised, eulogized, commended

Maimūn (مَيْمُون) Fortunate, auspicious

Maisarah (مَيْسَرَه) Ease, affluence, wealth

Mājid (مَاجِد) Glorified, exalted, noble, generous

Malbūb (مَلْبُوب) Highly intelligent

Mālik (مَالِك) Owner, proprietor, possessor, holder

Ma'mar (مَعْمَر) Inhabited, populated

Mamūn (مَامُون) Safe, secure, trustworthy, honest, faithful

Mansūr (مَنْصُور) Helped, advocated, defended,

Manzūr (مَنْظُور) Viewed, visible, visual, perspective

Maqbūl (مَقْبُول) Accepted, agreed to, admitted, received

Maqsūd (مَقْصُود) Intended, meant way, resolution

Marghūb (مَرْغُوب) Desirable, wished for, in demand

Marjān (مَرْجَان) Coral, red gem, beads, pearls

Mashhūd (مَشْهُود) Witnessed, attended, seen

Mashkūr (مَشْكُور) Loudable, thanked, worthy of thanks, praiseworthy

Masrūr (مَسْرُوْر) Happy, glad, joyous, jolly

Mas'ūd (مَسْعُوْد) Fortunate, lucky, happy

Māthil (مَاثِل) Standing, appearing, presenting oneself, to resemble

Mathīl (مَثِيل) Like, similar, identical, equal, picture

Matīn (مَتِين) Solid, strong, firm, durable, heavy, danty

Matlūb (مَطْلُوب) Claim, sought or desired object, wished for, wanted

Mazhar (مَظْهَر) Manifestation, expression, appearance, figure

Midh'ān (مِذْعَان) Submission, yielding, obedient, docile

Mikrām (مِكْرَام) Generous, kind, gracious

Munawwar (مُنَوَّر) Enlightened, illuminated,

bright

Miqdād (مِقْدَاد) One who breaks, cuts things

Miqdām (مِقْدَام) Intrepid, fearless, adventurous, first in attack

Mi'rāj (مِعْرَاج) Ladder, stair, steps

Misbah (مِصْبَاح) Lamp, bulb, light, burner

Mishāb (مِصْحَاب) Very obedient, compliant

Miskīn (مِسْكِين) Poor, pauper, miserable, humble

Mīthāq (مِيثَاق) Compact, alliance, covenant

Mithqāl (مِثْقَال) The weight, equal in weight, a coin

Moudūd (مَوْدُود) Wished for, beloved, desired

Mu'aiqīb (مُعَيْقِيب) Coming after, follower

Mu'awwidh (مُعَوِّذ) One who gives shelter, protection, asylum

Mu'ayyid (مُؤَيِّد) Helper, supporter

Mua'zzam (مُعَظَّم) Exalted, made great, glorified, honored

Mubārak (مُبَارَك) Blessed, lucky, fortunate, auspicious

Mubashshir (مُبَشِّر) Bringer of good news, harbinger, portent

Mubīn (مُبِين) Clear, plain, manifest

Muddaththir (مُدَّثِّر) Covered with, wrapped in

Mudhi'n (مُذْعِن) Submissive, yielding, tractable, docile

Muftī (مُفْتِي) An Islāmic lawyer who gives judicial decision, opinion

Mughīrah (مُغِيرَه) Attacker, aggressor, marauder

Mughīth (مُغِيث) Aider, one who gives succour

Muhādir (مُحَاضِر) Lecturer, lector, reader, speaker

Muhājir (مُهَاجِر) Emigrant

Muhammad (مُحَمَّد) Praised, praiseworthy, laudable

Muhīt (مُحِيط) Ocean, environment, perimeter, familiar with surrounding

Muhsin (مُحْصِن) Chaste, pure, virtuous

Muhsin (مُحْسِن) Beneficent, charitable, humanitarian

Muhtasib (مُحْتَسِب) Reckoner, taker of accounts

Mu'īd (مُعِيد) Repeater, reiterate, lecturer, assistant professor

Mu'izz (مُعِزّ) Bestower of honor, grace or glory

Mujaddid (مُجَدِّد) Renewer, originator, innovator, reformer

Mujāhid (مُجَاهِد) Struggler, freedom fighter

Mujammi' (مُجَمِّع) Collector, compiler

Mu'jib (مُعْجِب) Admirable, impressive, appealing, pleasant, delightful

Mukarram (مُكَرَّم) Honored, venerated, venerable

Mukhlid (مُخْلِد) Slow in becoming hoary

Mukhlis (مُخْلِص) Sincere, honest, loyal, devoted, constant

Mukhtār (مُخْتَار) Chosen, selected, fancy, excellent, superior

Mumtāz (مُمْتَاز) Excellent, first rated, fancy, fine, super

Mundhir (مُنْذِر) Warner, exhorter, cautioner

Munīb (مُنِيب) Repenting

Mun'im (مُنْعِم) Benefactor, beneficent

Munīr (مُنِير) Shining, brilliant, giving light

Munkadir (مُنْكَدِر) Muddy, turbid water

Muqaddas (مُقَدَّس) Sacred, divine, sanctified

Muqaddim (مُقَدِّم) Presenter,

donator, petitioner, brave, courageous

Muqarrab (مُقَرَّب) Close or intimate companion, favorite

Muqātil (مُقَاتِل) Fighter, combatant, warrior

Muqbil (مُقْبِل) Arriving, coming, approaching

Muqīm (مُقِيم) Inhabitant, remaining, living, dominated

Muqtadā (مُقْتَدٰي) Model, pattern, example, one who is imitated

Mu'āyyad (مُؤيَّد) Helped, supported

Murshid (مُرْشِد) Guide, leader, pilot, adviser

Murtada (مُرْتَضيٰ) Well pleasing

Mūsā (مُوْسي) Name of a Prophet ﷺ, caught from water

Musāhib (مُصَاحِب) Acompany, attendant, companion, comrade

Mushāhid (مُشَاهِد) Spectator, viewer, observer, watcher

Mūsir (مُوسِر) Rich, affluent, prosperous

Muslim (مُسْلِم) Muslim, believer peace loving

Mustajāb (مُسْتَجَاب) Completed with (request), answered (prayer)

Mustansir (مُسْتَنْصِر) The seeker of help, assistance

Mustanīr (مُسْتَنِير) Enlightened, illuminated

Mustaurid (مُسْتَوْرِد) Importer

Mutahhar (مُطَهَّر) Purified, sterilized, cleansed, purged

Mu'tasim (مُعْتَصِم) One who seeks the protection, defense

Mutayyab (مُطَيَّب) Perfumed

Muthannā (مُثَنّيٰ) A dual, double, dualized

Mutī' (مُطِيْع) Dutiful, loyal, devoted, pious

Mu'tib (مُعْتِب) One who reproves, censures

Muwahhid (مُوَحِّد) Unitarian, believer in the Oneness of Allāh

Muzaffar (مُظَفَّر) Victorious, conqueror, triumphant, winner

Muzzammil (مُزَّمِّل) Covered with, wrapped in

Wābil (وَابِل) Shower of rain, downpour

Nābit (نَابِت) Sprouting, germinating, new

Nadhar (نَذَر) To dedicate to good, to make a vow

Nadhīr (نَذِير) Warner, preacher, vowed, harbinger

Nadīr (نَضِير) Brilliant, shining, blooming, verdant

Nādir (نَاضِر) Moss, very green, flourishing

Nadr (نَضْر) Soft, beautiful, blooming, verdant

Nāfi' (نَافِع) Useful, helpful, beneficial

Nafī' (نَفِيع) Very useful, beneficial

Naihān (نَيْهَان) One who forbids, bans, interdicts

Na'īm (نَعِيم) Enjoying life, well being, blessed

Najm (نَجْم) A star, stemless plant, shrub, origin

Namīr (نَمِير) Delicious, pure, healthy, clear

Nāshī (نَاشِي) Youth, young man

Nāshit (نَاشِط) Nimble, active, energetic, lively, gay

Nāsih (نَاصِح) Advisor, counselor, exhorter

Nāsik (نَاسِك) Ascetic, anchorite, solitary, recluse

Nāsil (نَاسِل) Swift, haste

Nasīm (نَسِيم) Breeze, a soft movement of the air, zephyr

Nāsir (نَاصِر) Helper, defender

Nasīr (نَصِير) Helper, defender, advocate, champion

Nasr (نَصْر) Support, help,

succor

Nātiq (نَاطِق) Articulate, speaking, able to speak, radiant

Nayyir (نَيِّر) Shining, radiant, bright

Nazīl (نَزِيل) Guest, boarder, resident, occupant

Nāzir (نَاظِر) Viewer, supervisor, inspector, director

Nudār (نُضَار) Pure (of gold, silver)

Nūh (نُوح) Name of the Prophetﷺ, lamentation, one who consoles

Nu'mān (نُعْمَان) Blood, cattle, blessed

Nūr (نُور) Light, brightness, gleam, illumination

Qadhdhāfī (قَذَّافي) Catapult, rower, Ballisa

Q'aīd (قَعِيد) A companion in sitting, preserver, guardian father, locust

Qamar (قَمَر) Moon

Qāsif (قَاصِف) Touchy, thunder, roar

Qāsim (قَاسِم) Divider, distributor, divisor

Qasīm (قَسِيم) Participant

Qaswar (قَسْور) Lion, shooter, caster of weapons, hunter

Qawīm (قَوِيم) Right, straight, sound, orthodox

Qawwām (قَوَّام) Goodly nature, justness of proportion

Qayyim (قَيِّم) Manager, supervisor

Qurbān (قُرْبَان) Sacrifice, offering, companion of a king, immolation, host

Rabbānī (رَبَّاني) Pertaining to a master or lord, divine

Rabīb (رَبِيب) Reared, fostered, nourished

Rabīt (رَبِيط) Bound, ascetic, copular

Radā (رَضَا) Contentment, consent, acceptance, much desired object, prolonged hair

Rāfi' (رَافِع) High, to give dignity, elevation

Rafī' (رَفِيع) High, elevated

Rafīq (رَفِيق) Companion, comrade, friend

Rāghib (رَاغِب) Desirous, longing for

Rahīl (رَحِيل) Departure, migration, travel

Rahīm (رَحِيم) Compassionate, merciful

Rahīq (رَحِيق) The choicest, sweetest wine

Rahmat (رَحْمَت) Mercy, pity, compassion

Rā'ib (رَاعِب) Terrifying, causing fear

Raihān (رَيْحَان) Child, property, fragrant plant

Rajīl (رَجِيل) Walker, stern, firm

Rākib (رَاكِب) Rider, passenger on the board of a ship

Rāqib (رَاقِب) Watchman, observer

Raqīm (رَقِيم) Tablet, slab with an inscription, book

Rāshid (رَاشِد) Follower of the right way, guided

Rashīd (رَشِيد) To follow the right, be rightly guided

Rāsid (رَاصِد) Guard, watchman

Rāsikh (رَاسِخ) Firm, stable

Ratīb (رَطِيب) Humid, tender, fresh, delicate

Rāziq (رَازِق) Provider, one who furnishes with the means of living

Ribāh (رِبَاح) To obtain, profit, (name of the Prophet's servant)

Ridwān (رِضْوَان) Satisfaction, contentment, agreement

Rifā'ah (رِفَاعَه) Loudness, vehemence (of voice)

Rishād (رِشَاد) Right procedure, right guidance

Rishdah (رِشْدَه) A mode or

manner, noble

Riyād (رِيَاض) Gardens

Rouhān (رَوْحَان) Pleasures, fragrance

Sabbāh (صَبَّاح) Morning, early part of the day

Sabbār (صَبَّار) Very patient, tolerant

Sabhān (صَبْحَان) Beautiful, comely, bright

Sabīh (صَبِيح) Beautiful, handsome, comely

Sābiq (سَابِق) To race, compete, rival, precious, outstrip

Sābir (صَابِر) Patient

Sabīr (صَبِير) Patient, surety, chief

Sābit (سَابِط) Long haired, tall, of good stature

Sabūr (صَبُور) Patient, forbearing, long suffering

Sa'ādat (سَعَادَت) Happiness, felicity

Sa'd (سَعْد) Good luck, lucky

Sa'dān (سَعْدَان) A thorny plant, a tract, pasture

Sadāqat (صَدَاقَت) True, sincere, love, affection

Sādāt (سَادَات) Chief, lord, prince

Sadīd (سَدِيد) In the right direction, pursuing a right cause, true

Sādiq (صَادِق) True, sincere, veracious, truthful

Sadīq (صَدِيق) True friend, an intimate companion

Sadīs (سَدِيس) Sixth part, six years old, one of the teeth

Saffāh (صَفَّاح) The forgiving, one who forgives

Safīr (سَفِير) Ambassador, messenger, mediator

Safrān (صَفْرَان) Yellow, whistling

Safwān (صَفْوَان) Rock, soft and smooth stones

Sahāb (سَحَاب) Cloud, the

whole of a day

Sāhir (سَاهِر) Awake, to keep awaking

Sā'ib (صَائِب) Right, faultless, prudent, pertinent

Sa'īd (سَعِيد) Happy, blissful, auspicious

Siddīq (صِدِّيق) True, just, always veracious, charitable

Sā'im (صَائِم) Fasting, faster

Sā'iq (سَائِق) Driver, chauffeur, cheif

Sājid (سَاجِد) Humble, submissive, worshiper, prostrate

Sajjād (سَجَّاد) Extremely humble, simple, great worshiper

Sakhr (صَخْر) Rock, great mass of rock

Salam (سَلَم) Intact, antecedent, captive, surrender

Salāmah (سَلاَمَه) Safety, intactness, integrity, fitness

Sālih (صالح) Good, fit, just, virtuous

Salīk (سَلِيك) Traveler

Sālik (سَالِك) Traveler ordinary, polite

Salīm (سَلِيم) Sound, safe, without blemish

Sālim (سَالِم) Sound and safe, secure, intact, correct

Salkān (سَلْكَان) Arranged

Salmah (سَلْمَه) Tender, delicate

Salmān (سَلْمَان) Peace, intact

Samad (صَمَد) Lord, master, to remain firm, be steadfast, solid

Sāmī (سَامِي) High, lofty, exalted, sublime

Samīd (صَمِيد) Eternal, everlasting, firm

Sāmit (صَامِت) Silent, taciturn, soundless, speechless

Sārib (سَارِب) Appearing, going forth or away at random

Sārid (سَارِد) Stitcher

Sarīf (صَرِيف) Fresh milk, dry tree, a certain dye

Sārikh (صَارِخ) Crying out, shrieking, calling for help

Sārim (صَارِم) Cutting, sharp (sword), brave, energetic

Sāriyah (سَارِيَه) Column, pole, ship mast, a company, night rain

Sarmad (سَرْمَد) Perpetual, eternal, long night

Sa'ūd (صَعُود) Act of ascending, climbing

Sa'ūd (سَعُود) Prosperous, fortunate

Sayyib (صَيِّب) Having or pouring forth rain

Sha'bān (شَعْبَان) Imperfectly deal, the 8th month of the Islamic year

Shaddād (شَدَّاد) Strong, powerful, stout and sturdy

Shāfi' (شَافِع) Intercessor, petitioner, mediator

Shafī' (شَفِيع) Intercessor, mediator

Shāhid (شَاهِد) Eye witness, angel, evedentional example

Shākir (شَاكِر) Thankful, recognizer

Shakūr (شَكُور) Very grateful, thankful, recognizer

Shammās (شَمَّاس) Sunny, bright

Sharīb (شَرِيب) Addicted to drink, companion in drink

Sharīd (شَرِيد) Expelled, driven away

Sharīk (شَرِيك) Partner, associate, friend

Shāriq (شَارِق) Rising sun, shining, eastern side

Shihāb (شِهَاب) Brilliant star, shooting star, flame, alert

Shu'āib (شُعَيْب) Name of a Prophet عليه السلام, a repairer of cracks in wooden bowls

Shuraih (شُرَيْح) Long slice of meat, exposition, explanation

Sibt (سِبْط) Lank haired, tall, of good stature, children

Sibtain (سِبْطَيْن) Two grandchildren, the distinguished children

Sirāj (سِرَاج) Lamp, light

Subhān (سُبْحَان) Praise, exalted, high

Sulaik (سُلَيْك) Traveler

Sulaim (سُلَيْم) A little safe, sound, almost good

Sultān (سُلْطَان) Sultan, absolute ruler, command, empire

Surāqah (سُرَاقَه) Stolen

Suwaib (صُوَيْب) Right, correct

Tāb (طَاب) To please, delight, appealing to

Tabassum (تَبَسُّم) Smiling, smile

Tafaddul (تَفَضُّل) Superiority, preference

Tāhir (طَاهِر) Pure, clean, holy

Takrīm (تكْرِيم) Tribute, hospitality

Talhah (طَلْحَه) To be tired, fatigued, lean, banana tree, a kind of thorny acacia

Tālib (طَالِب) Student, seeker, pursuer, demander

Talīq (طَلِيق) Freed, emancipated, cheerful

Talq (طَلْق) Free, open, shot, gunshot, share, shackle

Tanvīr (تَنْوِير) Illumination, edification

Tanzīl-ur-Rahmān (تَنْزِيْلُ الرَّحْمٰن) Revealed or sent by the Compassionate (Allāh)

Taqī (تَقِي) Devout, pious, Godly

Tā'ib (تَائِب) Repentant, contrite

Tarīf (تَرِيف) Rich, affluent, opulent

Tāriq (طَارِق) Striker, visitor at night, morning star

Tasadduq (تَصَدُّق) Alms giving, beneficence

Tasnīm (تَسْنِيم) A brook, stream in Paradise

Turāb (تُرَاب) Earth, soil

Tawwāb (تَوَّاب) Most forgiving, merciful

Tayyār (طَيَّار) Swift, pilot, flier, airman, navigator

Tayyib (طَيِّب) Good, pleasant, agreeable, alive, nice

Thābit (ثَابِت) Firm, stable, permanent, established, still

Thaqalain (ثَقَلَيْن)Two worlds, two creatures, human being and jinn

Thāqib (ثَاقِب) Bright star, sharp, penetrating, shining

Thaqīb (ثَقِيْب) Very red like a flame of fire

Thamīr (ثَمِيْر) Fruitful

Thawbān (ثَوْبَان) To return, go back

Tawufīq (تَوْفِيق) Conciliation, harmonization, tuning

Tawhīd (تَوْحِيد) Belief in the Oneness of Allāh, monotheism

Tawqīr (تَوْقِير) Reverence, high regard

'Ubaid (عُبَيْد) Servant, slave, worshiper

'Ubaidah (عُبَيده) A humble servant

'Umair (عُمَيْر) Flourishing, cultivated, inhabited

'Umar (عُمَر) To live a long life, age, life span

Umayyah (اُمَيّه) Motherly, maternal

'Uqbah (عُقْبه) A mark, sign, turn, the last that remains

'Urwah (عُرْوَه) Loop, handle, buttonhole, environment of a town, tie

Uthrah (اُثْرَه) A mark, family honor and glory

'Uwaim (عُوَيم) A year, swimmer

'Uzair (عُزَير) To support,

strengthen

Waddāh (وَضَّاح) Bright day, beautifully white, clear, lucid

Wadīd (وَدِيد) Friendly, nice, affectionate

Wadūd (وَدُود) Lover, warm hearted, affectionate

Wahab (وَهَب) To donate, grant, bestow upon

Wahhāj (وَهَّاج) Intensely glowing, illuminated

Wāhib (وَاهِب) Grantor, donator, generous, liberal

Wahīd (وَحِيد) Unique, separated from others

Wāhid (وَاحِد) One, single, unique

Wā'id (وَاعِد) Promisor, promising

Wajīh (وَجِيه) Notable, dignitary, chief, prince

Wakīd (وَكِيد) Solid, sure, affirmed, confirm

Walīd (وَلِيد) Offspring, boy, slave, infant

Waqār (وَقَار) Gravity, dignified bearing, majesty

Wāqid (وَاقِد) To kindle, burn

Wārith (وَارِث) Heir, inheritor, successor

Warrāq (وَرَّاق) Paper maker, stationer, rich

Wāsif (وَاصِف) Praiser, one who describes

Wasīl (وَصِيل) An intimate companion

Wāsil (وَاصِل) To unite, bring together

Wathīq (وَثِيق) Strong, secure, tight, intimate friend, reliable

Wāthiq (وَاثِق) Self confident, convinced, sure, to make a covenant

Wāzin (وَازِن) Weigher, of full weight or quality

Warīth (وَرِيث) Successor, heir, inheritor

Yahyā (يَحْيٰ) The living, having means of subsistence

Ya'lā (يَعْلٰي) Elevated, high,

enacted

Ya'qūb (يَعْقُوب) Follower, successor, name of a Prophet عليه السلام

Yaqzān (يَقْظَان) Awake, watchful, cautious, attentive

Yasār (يَسَار) Easiness, facility

Yāsir (يَاسِر) To be easy, gentle with one, to take on left

Yazīd (يَزِيد) In excess, increase

Yūnus (يُونُس) Polite, affable, social, name of a Prophet عليه السلام

Yūsuf (يُوسُف) Name of a Prophet عليه السلام

Zafar (ظَفَر) Success, victory, having long nails

Qur'ānic Names for the Muslim Females

'Ābidah (عَابِدَه) Worshiper, adorer, obeyer

'Adīlah (عَدِيلَه) Excellent, generous, old, emancipated

'Ādilah (عَادِلَه) Fair, just, impartial

'Adīmah (عَدِيمَه) Lacking, wanting, having lost

'Adīnah (عَدِينَه) A piece or patch in the bottom of a bucket

'Adlah (عَدْلَه) Equal, seeker of just

'Āfiyah (عَافِيَه) Good health, soundness

'Ahīdah (عَهِيدَه) A confederate, bound by a covenant, old

Ahmarīn (اَحْمَرِين) Redness, brown

Ahwār (اَحْوَار) Having eyes intense black and white, beautiful

'Ainī (عَيْنِي) Eye witness, witnessed

'Ā'ishah (عَائِشَه) Alive, living, existent

'Ajīlah (عَجِيلَه) Hasty, speedy, quick

'Ākifah (عَاكِفَه) Engaged in, keeping to, occupied with

'Āliyah (عَالِيَه) High, elevated, sublime

Amān (اَمَان) To be safe, protected, guarantee, immunity, pact

'Amārah (عَمَارَه) Habitations and cultivation, a building, a tribe

'Amīlah (عَمِيلَه) Commercial correspondent, agent

Amīnah (اَمِينَه) Honest, true, loyal, faithful, constant, upright

Āminah (آمِنَه) A protector, believing woman

'Amīrah (عَمِيرَه) Inhabited, a flourishing state, well stocked

'Āmirah (عَامِرَه) Inhabitant, staying, abiding in a place

Ammarah (اَمَّارَه) Sign, instigator, inspirer

'Amrah (عَمْرَه) Necklace, head covering

Anīsah (اَنِيسَه) Genial, nice, friendly, sociable

'Aqīlah (عَقِيلَه) A noble woman, modest, highly esteemed

'Āqilah (عَاقِلَه) Intelligent, wise, comber of hair, heirs

Aqsā (اَقْصٰي) Farthest, remoter, more distant

'Irfānah (عِرْفَانَه) More knowing, knowledgeable

'Ārifah (عَارِفَه) Knowing, patient

'Arīj (عَرِيج) High, elevated, firmly executed affair

Arīkah (اَرِيكَه) Throne, couch, sofa

'Arīsh (عَرِيش) Booth, shed, carriage

'Āsifah (عَاصِفَه) Swift and violent wind, gale

'Asīmah (عَصِيمَه) Secure, defended, protected

'Āsimah (عَاصِمَه) Capital, defended, protected

Asmā (اَسْمَا) Height, grandeur, greatness, sign

'Ismat (عِصْمَت) Defense, protection, perseverance, sinlessness

'Ātifah (عَاطِفَه) Sentiment, affection, cause of inclining

'Atīqah (عَتِيقَه) Excellent, generous, old, emancipated

'Atiyyah (عَطِيَّه) Gift, grant,

donation, bonus

'Azīmah (عَزِيمَه) Determination

Azkā (اَزْكي) Thrive, cause to increase, pure, good

Bahjah (بَهْجَه) Joy, gladness, beauty, splendour

Baidā' (بَيْضَاء) White, clear, pure, silver

Baidah (بَيْضَه) An egg, helmet, white

Barīrah(بَرِيره) Pious, justified

Bārizah (بَارِزَه) Prominent, salient, important, embossd, in relief

Basharah (بَشَرَه) Skin, epidermis, surface cultic, generous

Basamah (بَسَمَه) Smile

Bāsimah (بَاسِمَه) Smiling

Basītah (بَسِيْطَه) Little, simple, modest

Bāzighah (بَازِغَه) Rising, bright

Birkah (بِرْكَة) Pool, basin, tank

Bisāt (بِسَاط) Wide, plain, carpet, rug

Bitānah (بِطَانَه) Living, inside, intimate friend, secret

Brakat (بَرَكَت) Blessing, happiness, abundance, prosperity

Bushrā (بُشْرٰى) Good news, good omen

Dahwah (ضَحْوَه) Early part of the day after sunrise, extending of the day

Damīrah (ضَمِيرَه) Secret thought, heart, grapes

Damrah (ضَمْرَه) To be lean, thin

Dāniyah (دَانِيَه) Approaching, coming, drawing near

Dhākirah (ذَاكِرَه) Memory, faculty of memory, one who remembers

Dhikrā (ذِكْرى) Remembrance, admonition, repentance

Duhā (ضُحٰى) Morning light, forenoon

Dujānah (دُجَانَه) Darkness, dark cloud, gloomy weather

Fadālah (فَضَالَه) A redundant, remaining portion

Fadīlat (فَضِيلَت) Virtue, excellence

Fā'iqah (فَائِقَه) Superior, excellent, surpassing

Fā'izah (فَائِزَه) Victorious, winner, a thing that rejoices

Fākhirah (فَاخِرَه) Glorious, excellence, costly

Fakīhah (فَكِيهَه) Mirthfulness, jetting, merriment

Farah (فَرَح) Joy, festivity

Fardah (فَرْدَه) Single, only, individual

Farhānah (فَرْحَانَه) Glad, rejoicing, happy

Farhīn (فَرْحِين) Rejoicing, glad, happy

Farīhah (فَرِيحَه) Rejoicing, joyful, delightful

Fārihah (فَارِهَه) Beautiful, comely girl, young woman

Farshah فَرْشَه)) A track, bed, mattress

Fasīhah (فَصِيحَه) Eloquent, chaste in language

Fatāhah (فَتَاحَه) Support, help

Fiddah (فِضَّه) Silver, para

Firdous (فِرْدَوْس) Paradise, garden

Fauziyah (فَوْزِيَه) Escape, success

Ghādiyah (غَادِيَه) A cloud that rises in the morning, rain in the morning

Ghafīlah (غَفِيلَه) Heedless, unmindful, soft, tender, verdant green

Ghairā (غَيْرٰى) Care for what is sacred, to avoid suspicion in jealous

Ghinā (غِنَا) Riches, luxury, song, chant

Habībah (حَبِيبَه) Attractive, beloved, well liked

Habrah (حَبْرَه) To embellish, make happy

Hadīqah (حَدِيقَه) Garden

Hādiyah (هَادِيَه) Guide, leader, guided

Hājirah (هَاجِرَه) Mid-day, noon, emigrant

Halīmah (حَلِيمَه) Gentle, patient, mild, gracious, clement

Hamdah (حَمْدَه) Praised, praiseworthy

Hamīdah (حَمِيدَه) Praised, deserving thanks

Hamīlah (حَمِيلَه) Shoulder belt of a sword, locket

Hamīmah (حَمِيمَه) Relation, intimate friend, cherished, hearty

Hamrā' (حَمْرَآء) Red, ruddy

Hanīfah (حَنِيفَه) Sincere Muslim, monotheist

Hāqqah (حَاقَّه) Right, truth, reality

Harīrah (حَرِيرَه) A piece of silk

Harrarah (حَرَّارَه) A woman trader of silk

Hāsin (حَاصِن) Chaste, virtuous

Hāsinah (حَاصِنَه) Chaste, virtuous

Hasnā' (حَسْنَآء) Good, fair, beautiful

Hasna (حَصْنَا) Chaste, virtuous, continent, married

Hassānah (حَسَّانَه) Fair, handsome, excellent

Hijāb (حِجَاب) To hide, cover, veil, prevent, intervene

Hisbah (حِسْبَه) Calculation, counting, reckoning

Hudā (هُدٰى) Direction, guidance in the right path

Humaira' (حُمَيْرَاء) Red, surname of 'Ā'ishah رضي الله عنها

Humādā (حُمَادٰى) Praised, praiseworthy, eulogized

Humrah (حُمْرَه) Redness, blush, dust of red brick

Husnā (حُسْنٰى) Handsome, better, good result, kindness

Ibrīq (اِبْرِيق) A beautiful, splendid and brilliant woman, pitcher

'Īmān (اِيمَان) Faith, creed, belief

'Imrānah (عِمْرَانه) The inhabited, well stocked land, a flourishing state

Isbāh (اِصْبَاح) Dawn, coming in the morning

'Ishrat (عِشْرت) Association, social fellowship

'Izzah (عِزَّه) Mighty, glorious, noble, prestige

Jabīn (جَبِين) Forehead

Jalīlah (جَلِيلَه) Lofty, sublime, venerable, significant

Jamīlah (جَمِيلَه) Beautiful, graceful, pretty, lovely

Kanzah (كَنْزَه) Treasure, buried treasure, gold, silver

Kāshifah (كَاشِفَه) Revelation, exposure, test

Karīmah (كَرِيمَه) Noble lady, precious object

Kawthar (كَوْثَر) A rich man, great blessing, a river in Paradise

Khāfiyah (خَافِيَه) Secret, hidden thing

Khā'ifah (خَائِفَه) Timid, fearing

Khaithamah (خَيْثَمَه) Having flat nose, broad ears

Khudrah (خُضْرَه) Greenness, verdancy, vegetables, greenery

Khālidah (خَالِدَه) Immortal, endless, perpetual

Khalīlah (خَلِيلَه) Intimate friend, comrade, sweetheart, lover

Khalīqah (خَلِيقَه) Creature, mankind, nature, meanness

Khansā' (خَنْسَاء) To hide, recede, retire

Khāshi'ah (خَاشِعَه) Humble, low, showing reverence,

ernest

Kawkab (كَوْكَب) Planet, star, a white spot in the eye

Kubrā (كُبْرٰى) Greatness, nobility, glory

Lā'ibah (لَاعِبَه) Player, sportswoman

Lailā (لَيْلٰي) Night, nocturnal, nightly, wise

La'ūb (لَعُوب) A sportful woman, playful, gamesome

Lubābah (لُبَابَه) The purest, prudent, rational

Lubainah (لُبَيْنَه) Milky, a little milk

Lubānah (لُبَانَه) Desire, object

Lubnā (لُبْنٰى) A tree found in Syria in abundance

Lubnah (لُبنَه) Milky, milk like

Matā' (مَتَاع) Goods, profits, personality

Mabshūrah (مَبشُورَه) A woman perfect in every respect

Mahdiyyah (مَهْدِيَّه) Rightly guided, presented, offered

Mahmūdah (مَحْمُوْدَه) Praised, praiseworthy

Mā'idah (مَائِدَه) Table, dining table, a sūrah in the Qur'ān

Maimūnah (مَيْمُوْنَه) Prosperous, lucky, blessed, auspicious

Mā'irah (مَائِرَه) One who brings, conveys

Mājidah (مَاجِدَه) Noble, glorious, illustrious

Malīkah (مَلِيكَه) Master

Manī'ah (مَنِيعَه) Impregnable, inaccessible, invulnerable

Mansūrah (مَنْصُورَه) Aided, supported, victor

Maqsūdah (مَقْصُودَه) Aimed at, desire, intended

Maqsūrah (مَقْصُوْرَه) Shortened, limited, bleached

Mardiyyah (مَرْضِيَّه) Well pleased

Marī'ah (مَرِيعَه) Rich in

pasturage

Marīhah (مَرِيحه) Exceedingly happy

Marwah (مَرْوَه) Name of a mountain in Makkah

Maryam (مَرْيَم) Mary, virgin, maidenhood

Māshiyah (مَاشِيَه) Walker, pedestrian, flocks, cattle

Mastūrah (مَسْتُوره) Hidden, concealed, invisible, marked

Ma'sūmah (مَعْصُومَه) Sinless, impeachable, unerring

Māziyah (مَازِيَه) Merit, excellence, superiority

Misbāh (مِصباح) Lamp, light, burner

Misbahah (مِسْبَحَه) Rosary, beads

Mu'azzamah (مُعَظَّمَه) Glorified, exalted, venerable, glorious

Mubashshirah (مُبَشِّرَه) Bearer of good news, preacher

Muhsinah (مُحْسِنَه) Beneficent, charitable, doer of good deeds

Mufīdah (مُفِيضَه) Abundant, overflowing, affluence

Mumtaz (مُمْتَاز) Excellent, distinguished, superb

Munawwarah (مُنَوَّرَه) Enlightened, bright, shining

Munīrah (مُنِيرَه) Shining, brilliant, bright

Muqaddas (مُقَدَّس) Sacred, holy, sanctified

Musarrat (مُسَرَّت) Joy, delight, pleasure, happiness

Mutahhirah (مُطَهِّرَه) Purified, cleansed, sterilized

Muznah (مُزْنَه) Rain, cloud

Nābitah (نَابتَه) Young woman, offspring, inexperienced

Nadīrah (نَضِيرَه) Brilliant, blooming, verdant

Nādirah (نَاضِرَه) Freshness, bloom, softness, verdant

Nādiyah (نَادِيَه) Caller, inviter

Nailah (نَيْله) Something obtained

Nā'ilah (نَائله) Attainer, winner, achiever

Nā'imah (نَاعِمَه) Soft, tender to the touch, fine, easy

Nā'imah (نَائِمَه) Sleeping, sleeper, lying down

Nājiyah (نَاجِيَه) Swift, saved, rescued

Nājiyyah (ناجِيَّه) A secret, confidential friend, swift

Najmah (نَجْمَه) Star, a stemless plant, shrub, origin

Najwā (نَجْوٰى) Secret communication, tribute

Nakhīlah (نَخِيلَه) Palm trees, dates, date palms

Nāshi'ah (نَاشِئَه) Young woman, juvenile, youthful

Nasīrah (نَصِيرَه) Helper, defender

Nāsirah (نَاصِرَه) Helper, protector

Nāsiyah (نَاصِيَه) Forepart of the head, forelocks

Ni'mat (نِعْمَت) Blessing, favor, mercy, grace

Nubdhah (نُبْذَه) A fragment, part, section, side, article

Nusrat (نُصْرَت) Succour, aid, assistance, triumph, victory

Qadamah (قَدَمَه) Bold, courageous, brave

Qa'īdah (قَعِيدَه) A female companion, sack, woven mat, wife, heap of sand

Qamrā' (قَمْرَاء) Moon-light, moon lit, bright

Qāni'ah (قَانِعَه) Contented, satisfied

Qānitah (قَانِتَه) A devout woman, pious, assiduous, prayer

Qarībah (قَرِيبَه) Near, closely related, neighbor

Qāsirah (قَاصِرَه) Modest, chaste

Qatīlah (قَتِيلَه) Martyred, killed, murdered

Qayyimah (قَيِّمَه) Upright position, firm, straight

Qidah (قِدَه) Good example, pattern, model for imitation

Qirtās (قِرْطَاس) Paper, a sheet of paper, a book

Quddūsiyah (قُدُّوسِيَه) Pure, very holy

Qudwah (قُدْوَه) A pattern, an exemplar, an object of imitation

Qumrah (قُمْرَه) Whiteness, greenish, white, a dingy white

Qurrat-ul-'Ain (قُرَّةُ العَيْن) Water-cress, darling, that by which the eye is refreshed

Qurshah (قُرْشَه) Bearing a bright, shining face

Rābi'ah (رَابِعَه) Fourth

Rājiyah (رَاجِيَه) Helpful, expecting for, looking forward

Rābihah (رَابِحَه) Successful, profitable

Rābiyah (رَابِيَه) Hill, mound, hillock, knoll

Rawdiyah (رَوْضِيَه) Verdant, blossoming, green

Rādiyah (رَاضِيَه) Content, satisfied

Rafāqat (رَفَاقَت) Good companions, friend

Rafī'ah (رَفِيعَه) Referred, high, elevated

Rāfi'ah (رَافِعَه) Raiser, a hard and elevated tract of land, elevated

Rafīdah (رَفِيدَه) Excellent supporter, aider, an assistant

Rāfidah (رَافِدَه) Timber supporting the roof, aid giver, supporter

Rāfiqah (رَافِقَه) Gentle, kind, a traveling companion

Raghībah (رَغِيبَه) Much desired object, generous, valuable gift, wealth

Rahīl (رَحِيل) Departure, travel, migration,

immigration

Rahīlah (رَحِيلَه) A she-camel strong to journey and strong to be saddled

Rāhilah (رَاحِلَه) Riding camel, traveler, emigrant

Raihānah (رَيْحَانَه) Fragrant plant of any kind, child, property, means of living

Rāji'ah (رَاجِعَه) Returning, coming or going back

Rajīlah (رجِيلَه) Firm and steadfast in walking

Rashīdah (رَشِيدَه) Rational, sensible, prudent, satisfied, with pleased, content

Rāshidah (رَاشِدَه) Adult, grown up, follower of the right, major

Ratībah (رَطِيبَه) To be fresh, tender, cool

Rawāsiyah (رَوَاسِيَه) Firmly fixed, immovable, mountain

Rawdah (رَوْضَه) Garden, meadow

Rabītah (رَبِيطَه) Tied animals, bound

Ridwānah (رِضْوَانَه) To be pleased, satisfied with, content

Rif'at (رِفْعَت) Elevation of rank, dignity, honor

Rummānah (رُمَّانَه) Pomegranate

Ruqayyah (رُقَيَّه) Ascent, the act of ascending

Sabā (سَبَا) Name of the city of Balqīs

Sa'bah (صَعْبَه) Difficult, hard, distressing

Sabāhat (صَبَاحَت) Beauty, comeliness

Sabbāh (صَبَّاح) Morning, early part of the day

Sabī'ah (سَبِيعَه) Seventh part, a seventh

Sabīhah (صَبِيحَه) Morning, bright

Sabīrah (صَبِيرَه) Patient, enduring, forbearing

Sābirah (صَابِرَه) To be patient, endure patiently

Sadāqat (صَدَاقَت) True, truthfulness, sincere friend

Sa'diyah (سَعْدِيَه) Fortunate, prosperous, happy

Safīhah (صَفِيحَه) Broad, flat stone, plate of metal

Safinah (سَفِينَه) Ship, boat, vessel

Safīrah (سَفِيرَه) Ambassador, mediator

Sahar (سَحَر) Early morning, dawn

Sahāb (سَحَاب) Cloud, the whole of a day

Sāhirah (سَاحِرَه) Sorceress, enchantress, witch

Sā'ibah (سَائِبَه) Left, forsaken, relinquished

Sa'īdah (سَعِيدَه) Fortunate, prosperous, happy

Sā'imah (صَائِمَه) Observing fast

Sā'irah (سَائِرَه) Walker, advancing, the remaining

Sājidah (سَاجِدَه) Humble, submissive, prostrate, worshiper

Sajjādah (سَجَّادَه) Prayermat, carpet

Sakhrah (صَخْرَه) Rock

Sakīnah (سَكِينَه) Calmness, quiet, tranquility

Salāmah (سَلاَمَه) Peace, quiet, perfection, free from faults and evils

Sālihah (صَالِحَه) Good, proper, good deed, fitting

Salimah (سَلِمَه) Stones, tender, delicate

Salamah (سَلَمَه) Tender, delicate

Salīmah (سَلِيمَه) Sound, intact, perfect, flawless

Salmā (سَلْمٰى) Safe, secure, free from evils

Salwā (سَلْوٰى) A certain salty meal granted to the children of Israīl

Sāmi'ah (سَامِعَه) Listener, hearer

Samī'ah (سَمِيعَه) Listener, hearer

Samīdah (صَمِيدَه) A lofty, hard elevated rock

Samīnah (سَمِينَه) A woman rendered fat or plump by nature

Sāmiyah (سَامِيَه) High, elevated, sublime, lofty

Sammā' (صَمَّاء) Rock, hard stone

Samrah (سَمْرَه) Evening or night entertainment

Samyā (سَمْيَا) High, elevated, great

Samiyyah (سَمِيَّه) High, any canopy covering over the head of a person

Sanā (سَنَا) Lightening, brilliance, radiance

Shāriqah (شَارِقَه) Shining, eastern side, side next to east

Sā'iqah (صَاعِقَه) Thunderbolt, death, deadly torment

Sarīrah (سَرِيرَه) Secret, mystery, hidden thought, heart

Sāriyah (سَارِيَه) Column, post, night-cloud, a company traveling at night

Saudah (سَوْدَه) A land in mountain where blackness prevails

Saumiyah (صَوْمِيَه) Fasting, fortress

Shafī'ah (شَفِيعَه) Intercessor, mediator, petitioner

Shāfiyah (شَافِيَه) Curing, healing, recovering

Shāhidah (شَاهِدَه) Eye witness, evidential example

Shāfi'ah (شَافِعَه) Intercessor, mediator, petitioner

Shakīlah (شَكِيلَه) Handsome, beautiful

Shākirah (شَاكِرَه) Thankful, grateful, appreciative

Shamsah (شَمْسَه) Necklace,

collar, kind of comb

Shārifah (شَارِفه) Honorable, dignified, noble

Shifā' (شِفَاء) To cure, heal, relieve from doubt

Shihābah (شِهَابَه) Brilliant star, shining, sharp, alert

Shifā (شِفَا) Brink, edge, border, cure, recovery

Siddīqah (صِدِّيقَه) True, just, righteous, charitable, friend

Sidrah (سِدْرَه) A lotus-tree

Sīmā (سِيمَا) Sign, mien, countenance, visage

Sughrā (صُغْرَى) Smaller woman

Suhailah (سُهَيْلَه) Easy, simple

Suhbah (سُحْبَه) A covering or film upon eye, remains of water in a pool

Sahlah (سَهْلَه) Smooth, soft, plain and level

Suknah (سُكْنَه) Peace and tranquility, ease

Sultānah (سُلْطَانَه) Love, affection

Sumairah (سُمَيْرَه) A partner in conversation by night

Sumayyah (سُمَيَّه) High, lofty, eminent

Sundus (سُنْدُس) Thin, fine silk

Sūrah (سُورَه) Sign, power

Tabassum (تَبَسُّم) Smiling, smile

Tābi'ah (تَابِعَه) Follower, successor, companion, disciple

Tāhirah (طَاهِرَه) Pure, chaste, innocent, virtuous

Tahrīm (تَحْرِيم) To proclaim sacred, unlawful

Tahsīn (تَحْسِين) Embellishing, adornment, approval

Tā'ibah (تَائِبَه) Repentant, penitent, contrite

Tajallā (تَجَلَّى) To become clear, plain, evident, manifest

Tal'at (طَلْعَت) Face, aspect

Tanwīr (تنوير) Enlightenment, illumination, edification

Tanzīlah (تَنْزيله) Bringing down, act of lowering

Taqdīs (تَقْدِيس) Sanctification, hollowing, conservation, dedication

Tasnīm (تَسْنِيم) To ascend, a fountain in Paradise, ride upon, advance

Tathīr (تَطْهِيْر) Purification, cleansing, sterilization

Tathmīn (تَثْمِين) Valuation, estimation

Tayyibah (طَيِّبَه) A good thing, pleasant, agreeable

Thabītah (ثبيته) Firm, established, certain, constant

Thālithah (ثَالِثَه) Third

Thaman (ثَمَن) Price, value of thing

Thamīn (ثَمِيْن) Costly, precious, valuable

Thamīnah (ثَمِينَه) Costly, valuable

Thāminah (ثَامِنَه) Eighth

Thamīrah (ثَمِيرَه) Profitable, productive, fruitful

Thamrah (ثَمْرَه) Fruit, knot at the end of a whip

Thamrīn (ثَمْرين) Fruit, gain, profit

Thāqibah (ثَاقِبَه) Bright, penetrating

Thawbānah (ثَوْبَانَه) A clothed woman

Tībah (طِيبَه) Lawfulness, willingness, goodness, blindness

Tūbā (طُوْبىٰ) Blessedness, happiness

Turfah (تُرْفَه) Ease, luxury, comfort

'Ubaidah (عُبَيْدَه) Female servant

Ufaq (اُفَق) Horizon, region, border

'Ulwah (عُلْوَه) The higher or highest part

Umāmah (اُمَامَه) Leadership,

dignity of an Imām, name of the Prophet's granddaughter

Umaimah (اُمَيْمَه) Mother, Guide

'Umrah (عُمْرَه) A visit, repairing of an inhabited place, pilgrimage

'Uqbā (عُقْبي) The end, last, consequence, result

Qurbah (قُرْبَه) Nearness of place, position or grade

'Urūj (عُرُوْج) To ascend, elevated, high

'Uyainah (عُيَيْنَه) A small spring, watcher, observer

'Uzlah (عُزْلَه) Hight, elevated, firmly executed affair

'Uzmā (عُظْمي) Great, immense, important, hard, terrible

Wafā (وَفَا) Faithfulness, devotion, faith, to pay the debt

Wāfiyah (وَافِيَه) Faithful, trustworthy, one who keeps her word

Wā'idah (وَاعِدَه) Unique, separated from others

Wahīdah (وَحِيدَه) One who makes a promise or an appointment

Wajāhat (وَجَاهَت) Consideration, dignity, authority,

Wājidah (وَاجِدَه) Finder, rich, possessing competence

Wajīhah (وَجِيهَه) Dignified, distinguished, handsome lady

Walīdah (وَلِيدَه) A young woman, a maid servant

Walījah (وَلِيجَه) Trust, resort, entrance

Wāqidah (وَاقِدَه) One who kindles (fire) lights (a lamp)

Wāqiyah (وَاقِيَه) Protector, preserver, defender

Wāsifah (وَاصِفَه) One who describes, qualifies, praises

Wasīlah (وَصِيلَه) Cultivation, fertility, friendship

Wāsilah (وَاصِلَه) To bring closer by affectionate conduct

Yāqūt (يَاقُوت) Corundum, ruby

Yasīrah (يَسِيرَه) Wealthy, affluent, faceable, easy

Yumainah (يُمَيْنَه) On the right, to the right

Yumnah (يُمْنَه) Blessed, prosperous, successful

Yusairah (يُسَيْرَه) Wealthy, prosperous

Yusrā (يُسْرَي) To be easy, docile

Zafīrah (ظَفِيرَه) Successful, triumphant

Zāfirah (ظَافِرَه) Victorious, triumphant, successful

Zafrīn (ظَفْرِين) Successful, victorious, lucky

Zāhidah (زَاهِدَه) Ascetic, virtuous, indifferent

Zahīrah (ظَهِيرَه) The point of mid-day, when the sun declines

Zāhirah (زَاهِرَه) Shining, bright, brilliant

Zahrā' (زَهْرَاء) Flower, bloom, beautiful lady, title of Fatimah ﷺ

Zākiyah (زَاكِيَه) Most virtuous, pure that which purifies, increases

Zakiyyah (زَكِيَّه) Pure, good, to grow, increase

Zarqā' (زَرقَاء) Blue, sky, heavens

Zihrah (زِهْرَه) Aid, assistance, support, help

Zill-i-Humā (ظِلّ هُمَا) Shadow of phoenix

Zubaidah (زُبَيْدَه) Selected, virtuous

Zubdah (زُبْدَه) Cream, prime, best part of a thing

Chapter:6

Islamic Names for the Muslim Males and Females

- Names Derived from History

Islamic Names for the Muslim Males

'Ābil (عَابِل) A bulky and strong man

'Ā'ith (عَائِث) The lion

'Asīb (عَسِيب) A straight and slender palm branch

'Āsij (عَاسِج) Slightly lame, to go at a quicker pace

'Ātim (عَاتِم) Tardy, late, sluggish

'Abrān (عَبْرَان) A compound of certain mixture

Abū Bakr (اَبُوبَكْر) To rise early, go forth in the morning

Abū Dujānah (اَبُوْدُجَانه) Of darkness, gloomy, rainy

Abū Sufyān (اَبُوْسُفْيَان) The wind that carries away dust, herbage

Abū Dhar (اَبُوْذَر) Scatterer, sprinkler of an atom

Abū Hurairah (اَبُوْهُرَيْرَه) Possessor of a kitten

Abyān (اَبْيَان) A man who dislikes or refrains from something

'Adās (عَدَاس) Traveler, energetic, observer

Adhfar (اَذْفَر) Having a pungent odor

Ādhin (آذِنْ) One who allows, gives permission

'Adī (عَدِي) The foot messenger of the sovereign, of a judge

Adīb (اَدِيب) Literary scholar, of polite manners, well bred

'Afāf (عَفَاف) A remedy, treatment

'Afar (عَفَار) A certain kind of tree

Affāq (اَفَّاق) Generous, to give one more than the other

Afīq (افِيق) Excelling in knowledge and generosity

Āfiq (آفِق) High blood, noble

'Āfir (عَافِر) Defiled with dust

'Afīr (عَفِير) Empty, barren, one who does not give a gift

Afrāhīm (اَفْرَاهِيم) Fruitful, affective, useful

Afrāsiyāb (اَفْرَاسِيَاب) Name of a popular Asian king

Āftāb (آفتاب) Sun, unique

Ahmas (اَحْمَس) Hard, vigorous, brave

Ahsan (اَحْصَن) Chaste, virtuous, to fortify, preserve

Ahwas (اَحْوَص) A man having contraction in his eyes

Ahyān (اَحْيَان) Occasionally, at times, time to time

Ārib (آرِب) Cunning, skilful, industrious

Ā'ib (آئِب) The clouds, returning

'Aidān (عَيدَان) A tall palm-tree, the tallest of palm-trees

Aimal (اَيْمَل) Hope, expectation, desire

'Aimān (عَيمَان) Desiring eagerly, longing for

'Āith (عَائِث) The lion

'Aithām (عَيْثَام) A species of white tall tree

Ajwad (اَجْوَد) Excellent, nose, bountiful, liberal

Akhram (اَخْرَم) Pool, one who hits the target, clever, hillock

Akhsham (اَخْشَم) Wide in the nose

Akhtar (اَخْتَر) Name of a star

Akhzar (اَخْزَر) To look at the side ways

Akwas (اَكْوَس) Intelligence, genius, clever, skilful

Akyas (اَكيَس) Clever, sharp,

intelligent

Al-Bāqir (ألباقر) The lion

Alīq (اَلِيق) To be bright, glittering, brilliant

Alīf (اَلِيف) To be friendly, accustomed to

Ālif (آلِف) To be familiar with, friendly

'Alīn (عَلِين) Open, overt, spread, manifest

'Alīth (عليث) Wheat mixed with barley

Almās (اَلمَاس) Diamond

Al-Mutawakkil (اَلْمُتَوَكِّل) One who depends upon Allah the Almighty

'Alqamah (عَلْقَمَه) Very bitter plant

Amān (اَمَان) Security, safety, protection

'Amīd (عَمِيد) Chief, leader, president, dean

Āmil (آمِل) Hoping, expecting

Amīm (اَمِيم) Beautiful in stature

Āmin (آمِن) Safe, secure, free

Amīn (اَمِين) One who trusts or confides in another

Āmir (آمِر) To command or multiply property or sons

'Amīs (عَمِيس) Intense matter

'Amīt (عَمِيْت) A twisted rope, clever and intelligent guardian

Amjad (اَمْجَد) More glorious, illustrious, glorified

Amlas (اَمْلَس) Smooth, sleek

Ānaq (آنَق) More rejoicing, pleasing,

Anas (اَنَس) To be polite, social, affable

Anīq (اَنِيق) Beautiful, pleasing, fragrant, a gift

Anīl (اَنِيْل) Innocent, inexperienced

Anīm (اَنِيم) Mankind, mankind and spirits

'Anīq (عَنِيق) To embrace

Anīs (اَنِيس) Friendly, gentle, polite

Anīth (اَنِيث) Plain, soft, even

Anjab (اَنْجَب) To be of noble family, commendable in looks, words or deeds

Anmār (اَنْمَار) Spotted white and black

Anmāth (اَنَمَاث) A thing mixed and moistened in water

'Annān (عَنَّان) Very fast, a great runner

'Ansal (عَنْسَل) A swift she-camel

Aus (اَوْس) The act of giving , gift or favor

'Aqadān (عَقَدَان) A species of dates

'Āqib (عَاقِب) A certain perfume, roots of the lotus tree

Ārām (آرَام) A beautiful, pretty

Arbad (اَرْبَد) Dust or ash colored, lion, dweller

Arbād (اَرْبَاض) Quarters, districts, ropes, a place of abode, an ostrich

'Arbān (عَرْبَان) Chaste, uncorrupt in speech

Ardān (اَرْدَان) The forepart of the sleeve or shirt, garment

Ardan (اَرْدَن) A sort of cloth

Artham (اَرْثَم) More fruitful and plentiful, abundant

Arīb (اَرِيب) Expert, skilful, intelligent and cunning

'Arīb (عَرِيب) Chaste, pure and uncorrupt in speech

'Ārid (عَارِد) Separate, secluded, alone

Arīd (اَرِيض) Fruitful, productive land

'Arīd (عَرِيد) Distant, remote, habit, custom

Ārid (آرِض) A soft or productive land, to remain on the ground

'Ārif (عَارِف) Chief, one who knows his companions

'Arīn (عَرِين) A wood, thicket,

abundant and dense trees

'Ārin (عَارِن) The lion

'Arīq (عَرِيق) Highborn, firmly established, ingrained

'Arīr (عَرِير) A stranger among the people

'Arīsh (عَرِيش) Booth, trellis for a grape vine, camel saddle for women, arbar

Ārīth (اَرِيث) The means of inflaming, kindling

Arjamand (اَرْجَمَنْد) Of a great value, exalted

'Armad (عَرْمَض) The green substance, a soft green

'Armaj (عَرْمَج) A certain plant, a sort of trees growing in soft plain land

Armāth (اَرْمَاث) A low gentle, soft voice

Armughān (اَرْمُغَان) Gift, favor, bestowal, bonus

Arqam (اَرْقَم) A certain serpent

'Arqān (عَرْقَان) Sweating

Arqash (أَرْقَش) Variegated with black and white

'Arrān (عَرَّان) A seller of the wood

'Arsaf (عَرْصَف) A certain plant found in Greece

Arsalān (اَرْسَلَان) Lion

Arsam (اَرْسَم) To tread upon the ground

Artal (اَرْتَل) Having beautiful teeth

Artam (اَرْطَم) He who keeps silence

Artāsh (اَرْتَاش) To be strengthened, a good state

Aryāsh (اَرْيَاش) Super or excellent clothing

Asad (اَسَد) Lion, brave

Asfah (اَصْفَح) Excessively wide in the forehead

Asfar (اَصْفَر) A great whistler

Ashāh (اَشَاح) An ornament worn by women

Ash'āth (اَشْعَث) Having the

hair disheveled

'Ashīb (عَشِيب) A country or a place of meadows

'Āshib (عَاشِب) A place of herb, producing meadows much

Ashja' (اَشْجَع) Courageous, brave, bold

Ashmat (اَشْمَط) Having whiteness in the hair

Ashraf (اَشْرَف) Elevated, dominate, to be high

Āsī (آسي) Physician, grief

'Asīd (عَصِيد) Twisted, turned, wreathed round

'Āsid (عَاصِد) A camel with a bended neck

'Āsif (عَاصِف) Swift, Sharp

'Āsil (عَاصِل) A hard and strong arrow

'Āsil (عَاسِل) A gatherer of honey from the hives, a wolf

'Asīr (عَسِير) Hard, difficult

'Asjad (عَسْجَد) Gold, gem, large camel

'Asalān (عَسَلَان) Disposition to nobleness

Asmar (اَسْمَر) Tawny, dusky, dark complexioned

'Ashwān (عَشْوَان) A species of dates, palm-trees

Āthif (آثِف) Firm, constant, following

Athīl (اَثِيْل) Firmly rooted, noble

Āthīr (آثِر) One who narrates a tradition

'Atīd (عَتِيد) Ready, prepared

'Ātif (عَاطِف) A she gazelle

'Atil (عَاتِل) A prefect, officer

'Ātin (عَاطِن) One who alights or descends in an abode

'Ātiq (عَاتِق) A young bird

'Ātir (عَاطِر) Fragrant, sweet smelling, odorous

'Attār (عَتَّار) Bold, courageous

Aurangzaib (اَوْرَنْگ زيب) Adorer of thrones, the title of a Mughal Emperor

Aus (اَوْس) An evergreen plant

'Awān (عَوَان) A cow, a beast of middle age

'Auf (عَوْف) State, condition, fortune

'Awīn (عَوِين) The aider, supporter, an armed attendant

'Awwām (عَوَّام) A swimmer, fleet (horse)

'Ayām (عَيام) Day time, a pleasant day

Ayāz (اَيَاز) Time of descending of a star, name of a Muslim governor

'Ayyād (عَيَّاض) A substitute, compensation

Azfar (اَزْفَر) A horse large in chest, belly

Azhar (اَزْهَر) Blossoming, blooming

'Azīb (عازِب) Distant, who goes away from his family

'Azzām (عَزَّام) Lion, resolute, determined

Bābar (بَابَر) Lion, an appellation of a Mughal ruler

Badhīm (بَذِيْم) Firm and steadfast, a strong man

Bādhil (بَاذِل) Generous, liberal

Bādhiq (بَاذِق) Cooked juice of grapes

Bādin (بَادِن) Big, bulky, big bodied

Badīn (بَدِين) Fat, bulky, big bodied

Bādir (بَادِر) Full moon, to hasten, run towards

Badr (بَدْر) Full moon, exquisitely beautiful person

Bāhir (بَاهِر) Overcoming in light

Bahrām (بَهْرَام) Mars, an ancient Persian king fond of zebra hunting

Bahzād (بَهْزَاد) Pious, virtuous, pure

Bārij (بَارِج) A large liberal disposition, sailor

Bājid (بَاجِد) Remaining, dwelling, staying

Bājis (بَاجِس) Flowing water

Bakhtāwar (بَخْتَاوَر) Lucky, fortunate

Bakhtiyār (بَخْتِيَار) Lucky, fortunate

Balta' (بَلْتَع) Skillful, expert

Bāqir (بَاقِر) Lion, who searches to the utmost knowledge, a collection of herb

Bāri' (بَارِع) Excelling in knowledge, courageous

Bārid (بَارِض) A tender plant or herbage

Birjīs (بَرْجِيْس) Jupiter

Bāsil (بَاسِل) Courageous, brave, strong on the occasion of fight

Basīl (بَسِيل) Courageous, brave, bold

Bāsim (بَاسِم) Smiling, happy

Bāsiq (بَاسِق) Tall, height

Basīr (بَصِير) Sharp sighted, intelligent

Basīt (بَسِيط) Spacious, a land of sweet smelling flowers

Basar (بَسَر) Anything fresh, juicy, moist

Basrah (بَصْرَه) Soft stones, inclining to white

Bassām (بَسَّام) Smiling

Bāsim (بَاسِم) Smiling much

Bāthiq (بَاثِق) A well full of water

Batīl (بَتِيل) Beautiful, slender, a limb, virgin

Bāzil (بَازِل) Who knows about good and evil, a she-camel that completes ninth year

Bihrōz (بِهْرُوز) A blessed day, lucky, fortunate

Bijād (بِجَاد) A stripped garment

Bilāl (بِلَال) Moisture, water, moisten

Bisān (بِصَان) Bright, glistering, beautiful

Bishām (بِشَام) A certain fodoriferous kind of tree

Binyāmīn (بِنْيَامِين) Lucky, fortunate

Buraidah (بُرَيْدَه) Courier, messenger

Burqān (بُرْقان) Shinning much in body

Busrah (بُصْرَه) Good red land

Dabīr (دَبِير) Secretary, writer, instructor

Dāfir (ضَافِر) Helper, assistant, supporter

Dāhīm (دَاهِيْم) The adorned crown

Daigham (ضَيْغَم) Lion, animal that bites

Daisān (دَيْصَان) One who declines or turns aside from the right course

Dājin (دَاجِن) An overspreading rain, an ewe,

Dālif (دَالِف) One who goes gently, leisurely

Dalīf (دَلِيف) One who walks with Short steps

Dāliq (دَالِق)Preceding, going before

Dalīs (دَلِيص) Water of gold, shining

Dam'ān (دَمْعَان) A bowl that is full so as to overflow

Damdām (ضَمْضَام) One who grasps every thing

Damīth (دَمِيْث) Soft and tender hearted, an even tract of land

Dāmid (ضامِد) Cleaving, holding fast

Dammām (ضَمَّام) One who collects seed produce

Damūm (ضَمُوم) Any valley between two hills

Dānish (دَانِش) Sagacity, understanding, knowledge

Darīr (دَرِير) Swift in running, compact and firm in make

Dāshāb (دَاشَاب) Favor, gift

Daumarān (ضَومَرَان) Sweet smelling plants, a wind

Dayyās (دَيَّاص) A man bulky and fleshy, strong

Dhahīb (ذَهِيب) Gilt, done over with gold

Dhakā' (ذَكَاء) Sharpness, acuteness of mind

Dhākhir (ذَاخِر) Fat, strongly built

Dhakiyy (ذَكِيّ) Sharp, intelligent, the age of completeness of strength

Dhakwān (ذَكْوَان) Bright, a kind of tree

Dhamalān (ذَمَلان) One who goes at a gentle pace

Dhamīl (ذَمِيل) A man who walks at a gentle pace

Dhamīr (ذَمِيْر) Courageous, clever, strong, beautiful man

Dhawwād (ذَوَّاد) A man who is a defender, protector

Dhawwār (ذوَّار) Envious, having a keen sense of honor

Dhihbān (ذِهْبَان) Water-gold, gold-powder mixed with size for ornamental writing

Dhuhaib (ذُهَيب) Gilded a little piece of gold

Dhuhbān (ذُهْبَان) Watergold, gold mixed in powder

Dhulfaqar (ذُوالْفَقَار) A spined sword

Dhuwaib (ذُوَيْب) Melted, dissolved, fluid

Dihyah (دِحْيَه) Commander in chief of army

Dilās (دِلَاص) Shining, glistening

Dilāwar (دِلَاوَر) Brave, courageous, bold

Dimād (ضِمَاد) Bandage, dressing for a wound

Dīmān (دِيمَان) Strongly built, swift, clever

Dimār (ضِمَار) A place, valley which conceals the traveler

Dimāth (دِمَاث) An even, soft

Dimām (ضِمَام) Thread, string, cord to chain things

Dīp (دِيْپ) Lamp, light

Dirghām (ضِرغَام) Lion, brave man, courageous to assault

Dujānah (دُجَانَه) A continuous and lasting rain

Dumrān (ضُمْرَان) A certain plant of the shrub kind

Fadālah (فَضَاله) Leftover, remainder, remains, excess

Fahd (فَهْد) Cheetah, hunting leopard

Fahīm (فهَيم) Very intelligent, having much understanding

Fuhair (فُهَيْر) Stone,

Fā'id (فَائِض) Generous, overflowing, abundant

Fā'ij (فَائِج) A wide tract of land, having beautiful long hair

Fā'iq (فَائِق) Excelling, surpassing

Fairūz (فَيْرُوْز) Turquoise (stone), brace, successful

Fajī' (فَجِيْع) To give pain, great calamity, disaster

Far'ān (فَرْعَان) Superior, excellent

Fārān (فَارَان) Name of a mountain

Farāz (فَرَاز) Spacious, high

Fardān (فَرْدَان) A single, an individual person or thing

Farghān (فَرْغَان) A wide, capacious vessel

Farhad (فَرْهَد) Fat, plump, compact in make, soft

Fāri' (فَارِع) Overtopping, surpassing

Fārid (فَارِد) A distinguished and unique

Fāris (فَارِص) Old, aged, advanced in age

Fārit (فَارِط) Preceding, going before, foremost

Fāriz (فَارِز) A tongue distinct, discriminating language

Farqad (فَرْقَد) The two stars in the constellation of the small bear that is near the pole star

Farrās (فَرَّاس) The lion, skillful, intelligent

Fartah (فَرْطَح) To expand, broaden, widen

Fasīh (فَصِيح) Eloquent, elegant speaker, chaste in language

Fasīh (فَسِيح) Spacious, roominess, wide

Fātik (فَاتِك) Bold, daring, one who does formidable affairs

Fatīn (فَتِين) A story tract

Fatīq (فَتِيق) Slit, rent

Fuwāq (فُوَاق) Milking, the time between two milkings

Fāzir (فَازِر) A soft wide and compact road

Fi'ām (فِئَام) A thing that is spread to sit upon

Fiyām (فِيَام) A piece of leather bucket, a company of men

Firād (فِرَاض) The mouth of a river

Firyād (فِرْيَاض) Wide, broad

Fitān (فِتَان) A leather covering

Fuljān (فُلْجَان) To retain water

Fur'ān (فُرْعَان) Superior, excellent

Gawhar (گَوْهَر) A pearl, gem, jewel, nature, descent

Ghadanfar (غَضَنْفَر) Lion, a man big or thick in body

Ghadīf (غَضِيْف) Relaxed, soft, plentiful in circumstances

Ghādif (غَاضِف) Soft, plentiful, relaxed

Ghafīr (غَفِيْر) Large, great, covering, guard

Ghailān (غَيْلَان) Bulky, big splendid

Ghaimān (غَيْمَان) Thirsty, affected with internal heat

Ghayyūr (غَيُّوْر) Very jealous, sensitive

Gulbār (گُلْ بَار) Shedding flowers, scintillating stick

Gulfām (گُلْفَام) Rosy faced, red colored

Gulraiz (گُلْ ریز) Shedding flowers, a kind of firework

Gulzaib (گُلْ زیب) Handsome, flower like

Gulzār (گُلْزَار) A bed of roses, a garden, well populated town

Habāb (حَبَاب) Bubbles, dew drops, utmost power, glow worm

Habīr (حَبِير) A kind of garment

Hādhir (حَاذِر) Cautioner, fearful

Hadhīr (حَذِير) Cautioner, one who gives warning

Hādir (حَادِر) A rope strongly twisted

Hadīr (حَضِير) A strongly twisted rope

Hāfid (حَافِد) Active, servant, assistant

Hāfir (حَافِر) Digging, a digger

Hafīr (حَفِير) A newly dug well, cleared out

Hafs (حَفْص) Lion, a small home

Haider (حَيْدَر) The lion, brave

Hājib (حَاجِب) Chamberlain, door keeper, attendant, eye brow, edge of anything

Humāyūn (هُمَايُون) Fortunate, blessed, emperor, august

Hamās (حَمَاس) Hardness, firmness

Hamadhān (هَمَذَان) Quick, swift, sharp

Hamīj (هَمِيج) Sacred doe, antelope, frightened people

Hāmij (هَامِج) The people who left to mix tumultuously

Hamīr (هَمِير) Beautiful gazelle

Hāmir (هَامِر) Loquacious, a great talker, pouring rain and tears

Hamīs (حَمِيْس) Brave, bold, a strong hearted man

Hamīs (هَمِيس) Who speaks in a gentle or soft manner

Hāmit (حَامِت) Sweet, gentle, mellifluous, firm

Hamīz (هَمِيْز) Wise, intelligent, courageous, bold

Hammām (هَمَّام) Hero, generous, liberal

Hammās (حَمَّاس) Courageous, brave, bold, a guard

Hammās (هَمَّاس) A strong and vehement lion

Hamnān (حَمْنَان) Small sticks, black berry

Hamzah (هَمْزَه) The sound character

Hanbal (حَنْبَل) Fleshy, short

Hanīn (حَنِيْن) Cry of compassion, emotion, fond of affection

Hannād (هَنَّاد) One who fails, comes short of

Hafīr (حَفِير) A newly dug well, cleared out

Hanūn (حَنُوْن) Compassionate, soft hearted

Hanzalah (حَنْظَلَه) A certain bitter plant, colocynth

Harīd (هَرِيد) A garment, piece of cloth

Hārith (حَارِث) A collector of property, farmer

Hārithah (حَارِثَه) One who strives, a collector of property

Harīz (حَرِيز) Fortified, preserved with care, valued

Hāriz (حَارِز) Protected, safe

Hasān (حَصَان) Chaste, continent, abstaining from what is unlawful

Hashīb (حَشِيب) A thick rough garment

Hāshid (حَاشِد) Equipped

Hashīm (حَشِيْم) Modest, bashful, revered, regarded with awe

Hashīm (هَشِيم) Crushed, dry and brittle, hay, stubble

Hāshim (هَاشِم) Generous, liberal, one who crushes or breaks

Hashmat (حَشْمَت) Reverence,

modesty, bashfulness, awe, anger

Hasil (حَسِيْل) A young calf

Hasīl (حَصِيل) A certain plant

Hāsim (حَاسِم) Consecutive, continuous

Hasīm (حَسِيم) Anything made consecutive

Hāsin (حَاسِن) The moon, becoming good

Hāsin (حَاصِن) Abstaining from what is unlawful, chaste

Hasīn (حَصِين) Unapproachable, strongly fortified

Hātim (حَاتِم) A judge, one who decrees, generous, bold

Hazīm (حَزِيْم) Prudent, resolute, firm

Hazīz (هَزِيز) Briskness, pace, manner, sprightliness

Hazzāl (هَزَّال) Leanness, thinness, emaciation

Himas (حِمَاس) Enthusiasm, bravery, vigorousness in ones belief

Hirran (حِرَّان) To become restive, stop

Hisbān (حِسْبَان) Estimation, supposition

Hishām (هِشَام) Generosity, liberality

Hashshām (هَشَّام) Generosity, liberality

Hizām (حِزَام) Belt, girth, swaddling bands

Hudair (حُضَير) Urban, citizen, town man

Hudhāfah (حُذَافَه) Clipping or what one cuts off

Hudhaifah (حُذَيْفَه) Easy, soft

Humād (حُمَاد) A purpose, the ultimate objective, strife

Humaid (حُمَيْض) A rose having red flowers

Humāris (حُمَارِس) Courage, boldness, defence

Hummād (حُمَّاض) Eager, desire for anything

Humrān (حُمرَان) Red garment

Hurairah (هُرَيْرَه)A cat, kitten

Hurān (حُران) To become restive, stop

Husām (حُسَام) Sharp sword, edge of sword, blade,

Huwayyasah (حُوَيَّصَه) Narrow-eyed, having one eye smaller than the other

'Ibāl (عِبَال) The mountain rose

'Ibān (عِبَان) The time, season of a thing

Ibrīz (اِبْرِيز) Pure gold

Ibtisām (اِبْتِسَام) Smile

Idh'ān (اِذْعَان) Submission

'Ifās (عِفَاص) The receptacle of money, piece of rag

'Ihād (عِهَاد) Recent, rains

Ihtisham (اِحْتِشَام) Bashfulness, modesty, reverence

'Ikās (عِكَاس) The cord, to render submissive

'Ikrish (عِكْرِش) Quack grass, couch grass

'Ikramah (عِكْرَمَه) Pigeon

Ilyās (اِلْيَاس) Affected by pathisis or consumption

'Īmār (اِيمَار) To multiply property, sons or camels

Imlīs (اِمْلِيس) Quick, swift, excellent

Imyāth (اِمْيَاث) One who steeps a thing in water

'Inān (عِنَان) The side of the house, bridle, lofty region of the sky

'Ināyat (عِنَايَت) Care for, manage, solicitude

Inbisāt (انبِسَاط) Joy, cheerfulness, happiness

Inshād (اِنْشَاد) To recite poetry, raise in fame

'Iqās (عِقَاص) Locks hanging down from the head

'Irān (عِرَان) A piece of wood, stick

'Īran (عِيرَان) The lion

'Irbād (عِرْبَاض) Hard and strong, thick

Irbāth (اِرْبَاث) To be restrained, stopped

Irbiyān (اِرْبِيَان) A species of white fish

'Irfān (عِرْفَان) Lofty, exalted, generous

Irhān (اِرْهَان) A rope, thong of a yoke, strap

'Irmād (عِرْمَاض) The green substance, herb

'Irsāf (عِرْصَاف) The pegs or pins for a camel's saddle

Irti'ām (اِرْتِئَام) A consolidated, twisted one

Irtisāf (اِرْتِسَاف) Raised, elevated

Irtisām (اِرْتِسَام) One who endeavors, remembers repeatedly, stick to a manner or a thing

'Irzāl (عِرْزَال) Lion's lair, booth constructed on a tree

'Isāl (عِصَال) Strong, hard and crooked

Ishāh (اِشَاح) An ornament worn by women

Ishtiyāq (اِشْتِيَاق) Strong desire, ardent longing, passionate to love

Isrān (اِصْرَان) The ear hole

'Itbān (عِتْبَان) One who reproves a man for evil conduct

Iyād (اِيَاد) A compensation, substitute, means to defend

'Iyān (عِيَان) Clear, evident, open, manifest

'Iyās (عِيَاص) Confused and intricate

Iyās (اِيَاس) The act of giving

Izhār (اِزهَار) Blossoming, blooming

'Izlān (عِزْلَان) A species of locust

Jabalah (جَبَله) Natural form, temper, constitution

Jābar (جَابَر) He who sets broken bones, who forces,

compels

Jabīr (جَبِيْر) He who compensates, repairs, make amends for

Jabrān (جَبْرَان) One who restores or incites to restore a thing to its place

Jādhib (جَاذِب) Attractive, attracting powerfully

Jadhīl (جَذِيْل) Abundant, much, intelligent, eloquent

Jādhil (جاذِل) Firm, erect in place, steadfast

Jadhlān (جَذْلَان) To rejoice, make merry

Ja'far (جَعْفَر) River, stream

Jahāngīr (جَهَانْگِير) World conqueror, appellation of a Mughal emperor

Jahānzaib (جَهَانْزِيب) World adorning, high, strong voice, beautiful, one who pleases the beholder

Jahīr (جَهِير) Loud, vehement, bold, daring

Jāhir (جَاهِر) He who reads, recites a thing aloud

Jamshīd (جَمشيد) A reputed king of Persia, inventor of medicines

Jundal (جُنْدَل) Large stone, water fall

Janīb (جَنِيب) Followers, an intimate friend

Jarīd (جَرِيْد) Branch of a palm-tree, whole or complete year

Jarrār (جَرَّار) Bold and brave, commander

Jarīr (جَرِير) A cord of leather , rope, one who pulls

Jathīr (جَثِير) The quiver of shins

Jawwād (جَوَّاد) Generous, liberal, kind

Jāzil (جَازِل) Cheerful, intelligent, sound in judgment

Jāzim (جَازِم) A full water skin

Jimām (جِمَام) To become, abundant, much

Jouhar (جَوْهَر) Jewels, pearls, substance, soul, excellence

Julaibīb (جُلَيْبِيب) Importer, driver

Jumām (جُمام) To become abundant, much

Jumān (جُمَان) Beads made of silver, like pearls

Jundub (جُنْدُب) A species of locust, grasshopper

Kabshah (كَبْشَه) A handful, hook and eye, name of the Prophet's servant

Kāmin (كامِن) Latent

Kāshir (كَاشِر) Displaying of one's teeth in laughing

Kathīb (كَثِيب) A sand hill

Khabbāb (خَبَّاب) The ambling pace, swiftness

Khābir (خَابِر) One who tests, proves things, experienced

Khabūr (خَبُوْر) A lion, courageous

Khadhdhām (خَذَّام) Sharp, swift

Khādib (خَاضِب) One who dyes his hair

Khadīb (خَضِيب) Anything dyed, colored

Khalīs (خَلِيْس) Courageous, clever, swift, sharp

Kāmrān (كَامْرَان) Successful, achieving ones wish

Khārif (خَارِف) The keeper, watcher of palm-trees

Khāriq (خَارِق) A sharp, cutting sword

Khashīb (خَشِيب) Picked out, selected, big, rough

Khāshib (خَاشِب) One who eats what he can

Khāshif (خَاشِف) Water freezing, brisk and lively, sprightly

Khashīf (خَشِيف) Swift, quick, water freezing

Khath'am (خَثْعَم) The lion, determined to help

Khathīm (خَثِيْم) Wide and round, spread

Khāwar (خَاوَر) The east, hailing from the east

Khāzim (خَازِم) A cold wind

Khazīr (خَزِير) A certain kind of food

Khibān (خِبَان) Folded garment

Khilās (خِلَاس) Bold, swift

Khimās (خِمَاص) Hungry

Khubaib (خُبَيْب) Lofty, elevated, high

Khubān (خُبَان) One who folds and sews the clothes

Khudhaimah (خُذَيْمَه) To make an arrangement

Khufāf (خُفَاف) Light weight, nimble, prompt, insignificant

Khuraim (خُرَيْم) Happy, cheerful, rejoicing

Khurshīd (خُورشِيْد) Sun

Khurram (خُرَّم) Glad, cheerful, a certain kind of a plant

Khushām (خُشَام) A man having a large nose, a long and prominent mountain, the lion

Khushnūd (خُوشْنُود) Happy, pleased, glad

Kurz (كُرْز) Cherry, shepherd's bag

Labīd (لَبِيد) A sack, folder, bag

Labīn (لَبِين) Abundant in milk, lover of milk

Labīq (لَبِيق) Skilful, intelligent, elegant, fitting well

La'īq (لَئِيق) Efficient, intelligent, clever, swift

Laith (لَيْث) Lion

Lāsiq (لَاصِق) An associate, a devoted companion

Lasīq (لَسِيق) Close companion, adherer

Liāqat (لِيَاقَت) Competence, worthiness, fitness, decency

Libān (لِبَان) To conciliate, mollify

Liyāh (لِيَاح) Intensely white, a white bull

Mirdās (مِرْداس) Road roller, steam roller, roller

Mahīd (مَهِيد) Pure butter

Mahnūn (مَهْنُون) Strong, healthy, powerful

Mahrū (مَهْ رُو) Beautiful like moon

Mā'id (مَائِد) A branch succulent and tender

Ma'īd (مَئِيد) A branch, fresh, tender, supple

Mā'ih (مَائِح) A tooth stick, one who descends in water to fill a bucket

Mā'ij (مَائِج) A sea in a state of commotion

Mā'ir (مَائِر) One who brings, conveys, provides

Mā'is (مَائِس) One who walks in self conceited gait

Maithām (مَيْثَام) A white tree, a certain sort of food

Makhāriq (مَخَارِق) A wide desert, wide land

Makhrafah (مَخْرَفَه) A garden of palm-trees, a single palm tree

Malhān (مَلْحَان) A sucker

Malīh (مَلِيح) Witty, salted, goodly, fine, pretty

Malīl (مَلِيل) Exhausted, fatigued

Mamnūn (مَمْنُون) Much obliged, weak, languid, limit

Māmūn (مَامُون) Trustworthy

Manī' (مَنِيع) Immune, invincible, well fortified

Manshā' (مَنْشَاء) The place of origination of anything

Ma'qil (مَعْقِل) Fortress, refuge, high mountain

Marārah (مَرَارَه) Bitterness, loathing, gall bladder

Marhān (مَرْحَان) Brisk, lively, sprightly

Māris (مَارِس) One who strives, struggles to obtain

Mārit (مَارِط) A man having scanty hair

Marthad (مَرْثَد) A generous man, the lion

Marwān (مَرْوَان) A hard rock

Marzubān (مَرْزُبَان) Chief, a courageous cavalier

Matīn (مَتِين) Strong, solid, robust

Maujān (مَوْجَان) A dashing state of sea, water

Mazīz (مَزِيز) To be exalted, lofty, superior

Mid'am (مِدعَم) A means of supporting, staying

Mihjan (مِحْجَن) A crooked, hooked, staff or stick

Mihrān (مِهْرَان) Skilful, dexterous, expert

Mihrjān (مِهْرَجَان) A feast of the Persians

Mihyān (مِحْيَان) The time or season of a thing

Mikhnaf (مِخْنَف) Knife, blade, cutter

Mirbā' (مِرْبَاء) An elevated place of observation

Mirdās (مِرْدَاس) A great mountain

Misbāh (مِصْبَاح) A lamp, lighted wick

Miswar (مِسْوَر) A leathern pillow

Mi'wān (مِعْوَان) Supporter, helper

Mu'āwiyah (مُعَاوِيَه) One who leads, drives

Mubādir (مُبَادِر) Precocious

Mubārak (مُبَارَك) Blessed, beautified, felicitated

Mubtadir (مُبْتَدِر) Lion, the first to assault

Mihsan (مِحْصَن) A lock, basket, the clasps

Muhtashim (مُحْتَشِم) Modest, chaste, shy, bashful

Mu'īl (مُعِيْل) A man having numerous family, household

Mujāshi' (مُجَاشِع) Extremely terrified, greedy

Mukhtashib (مُخْتَشِب) One who eats what he can

Munīf (مُنِيف) High, lofty mountain, high nobility

Murrah (مُرَّه) Bitter

Murshiq (مُرْشِق) Having a stretched out or long neck

Murzim (مُرْزِم) Firm, steadfast, upon the ground

Mus‘ab (مُصْعَب) An unbroken camel, a stallion, a man whose camel is refractory

Musayyab (مُسَيَّب) Free, willful

Musharraf (مُشَرَّف) Honorable, venerable, honorific

Mushrif (مُشْرِف) Projecting, overlooking, commanding, close to

Mushtāq (مُشْتَاق) Ardently longing, deeply desiring, yearning

Musīb (مُصِيب) Right, correct, hitting the mark

Mūsir (مُوسِر) Rich, affluence, easy liver

Mutaz (مُتاز) Strong, exalted

Mu‘tib (مُعْتِب) One who is reluctant, hesitant

Nab‘ān (نَبْعَان) The two shafts of a cart

Nābi‘ (نَابِع) A certain tree, spring, sweat

Nabīdh (نَبِيذ) Wine, thrown away, spurned

Nābigh (نَابِغ) Distinguished man, genius, superior

Nabīgh (نَبِيغ) A distinguished man, genius, superior

Nabīh (نَبِيه) Eminent, celebrated , well-known

Nabīj (نَبِيج) Cloud, vehement voice

Nabīl (نَبِيْل) Generous, noble minded, skilled archer

Nabīt (نَبِيط) Depth, common people

Nabīth (نَبِيث) The raised dust, clay

Nadī (نَدِي) The rainbow, cooked, baked

Nādil (نَادِل) Solid, one who draws out

Nadīm (نَدِيم) Intimate friend, companion, comrade

Nādir (نَادِر) A rare thing, rarity, unusual

Nādis (نَادِس) Intelligent, wise, swift

Nāfidh (نَافِذ) Efficacious, affective, skilful

Nafih (نَافِح) Diffusing odor, fragrant, cloud full of rain

Nāfij (نَافِج) A cloud full of rain

Nafīs (نَفِيس) Sought after, precious, valuable

Nāfith (نَافِث) Enchanting, pleasing

Nahīs (نَهِيص) Shining, brilliant

Nahīd (نَهِيْد) Cream, fresh butter

Nāhid (نَاهِد) To attack, assault on enemy

Nahīk (نَهِيْك) A brave man, courageous, bold

Nāhiz (نَاهِز) Approaching the time of weaning

Nuhlān (نُهْلَان) Thirsty, satisfied with drink

Naihān (نَيْحَان) To shake or move a branch

Nā'il (نَائِل) Something obtained, gained

Nā'im (نَاعِم) Soft, tender to the touch, fine, delicate

Nā'ir (نَائِر) Apparent, manifest, beautiful in color

Nāi's (نَائِص) Raising head, running away at random

Nā'is (نَائِس) Threads hanging down and moving about

Naisabān (نَيْسَبَان) A straight and direct way

Najīb (نَجِيب) Noble, of noble family, superior

Najīd (نَجِيد) The lion, sweating by reason of work

Najīh (نَجِيح) Patient, judicious

Nājil (نَاجِل) A noble family, of good breed

Nājish (نَاجِش) A pursuer, ensnares

Nājiz (نَاجِز) Coming to an end, last, perishing

Namīr (نَمِير) Sweet and wholesome water

Namīs (نَمِيص) Cropped grass, pulled out hair

Nāmūs (نَامُوس) Astute, law, code

Naqiyy (نَقِي) Pure, clean, innocent

Nardin (نَرْدِن) Sweet smelling plant

Narmīn (نَرْمِين) Soft, delicate, smooth

Nashā' (نَشَآء) A young man, an excellent youth

Nāshib (نَاشِب). Sticking fast in a thing, possessing arrows

Nashīd (نَشِيد) Elevation of the voice

Nāshid (نَاشِد) A man who gives information

Nasī' (نَصِيع) Manifest, pure white, clear

Nāsi' (نَاصِع) Manifest, clear evident, pure white

Nasīb (نَسِيب) A relative, kinsman

Nasīf (نَسِيف) A secret, foot mark, obscure

Nasīh (نَصِيح) One who counsels sincerely, faithfully

Nāsih (نَاصِح) One who counsels sincerely, faithfully

Nathīl (نَثِيل) The dust, the foundation of house

Nāthir (نَاثِر) To shake off unripe dates

Nātis (نَاطِس) A spy who searches for news, tithing

Nawās (نَوَاس) One who struggles with or undertakes any matter

Nāwash (نَاوَش) One who

grasps, seizes, grants a favor

Nawāz (نَوَاز) Cherishing, soothing, caressing, dangling, swinging

Naufal (نَوْفَل) Sea, present, handsome, liberal, lion's cub

Nawīd (نَوِيد) Good news, invitation to a wedding

Naushād (نَوْشَاد) Beautiful, handsome, dangling, swinging, pendulous

Nawwās (نَوَّاس) Quivering and flaccid

Nāyāb (نَايَاب) Rare, matchless

Nayyir (نَيِّر) Bright, shining

Nāzih (نَازِح) A remote and distant dwelling

Nazīh (نَزِيح) Remote, distant dwelling

Nazīh (نَزِيه) Excellent in manners, noble

Nāzim (نَاظِم) Organizer, adjuster

Nāzir (نَاظِر) A guardian, watcher, apple of the eye

Nibrās (نِبْرَاس) A lamp, light

Nidār (نِضَار) Pure gold, silver

Nighrān (نِغْرَان) Certain birds, sparrows

Nihāl (نِهَال) Thirst, satisfied with drink, glad

Nihās (نِحَاس) A natural disposition or temper

Nimār (نِمَار) Leopard

Nīshān (نِيشَان) A decoration, medal, mark

Nishdān (نِشْدَان) One who seeks after, informs about a stray beast

Nitāb (نِطَاب) The head, tendon of the neck

Nithār (نِثَار) To disperse, disseminate, sacrificed

Nuhlān (نُهْلَان) Gift, present

Owais (أُوَيْس) Small gift, wolf, one of the tribes of Madinah, gravitation

Qabīn (قَبِين) Sharp, intelligent

Qābis (قَابِس) The taker of fire

Qabīsah (قَبيصَه) A little thing

Qābūs (قَابُوْس) Beautiful, handsome

Qadīd (قَدِيد) A garment, piece of cloth, thick garment

Qais (قَيْس) To compare, judge, measure something by another

Qaisar (قَيْصَر) King, the Roman king

Qā'it (قَائِت) The lion, one who feeds

Qalbar (قَلْبَر) Crested lark

Qāmis (قَامِس) One who strikes, kicks with the foot

Qamīs (قَمِيس) Diver for pearls

Qammās (قَمَّاس) A diver, diver for pearls

Qanbar (قَنْبَر) Thick garment, a species of bird

Qanīb (قَنِيب) Dense cloud, companion

Qā'qā' (قَعْقَاع) To clatter, rattle, clank

Qāris (قَارِس) A cold day

Qasām (قَسَام) Beauty, intense heat, divider, distributor

Qasfān (قَصْفَان) Crowding together of people

Qasīb (قَسِيب) A current or flow of water

Qāsih (قَاسِح) A hard and strong lance, spear

Qashīb (قَشِيب) White, clean, polished, new, rusty, poisoned food

Qatādah (قَتَادَه) A thorny tree

Qawwām (قَوَّام) One who rises in the night to offer prayer

Qudā'ah (قُضَاعَه) Leopard, leopard like animal

Qināb (قِنَاب) The claw of the lion, the string of a bow

Qudaid (قُدَيْد) A piece of cloth, thick garment

Qudāmah (قُدَامَه) A man of eloquent speech

Qutbah (قُطْبَه) Stitch, axle

tree, axis, pivot

Rā'i' (رَائع) Swift, excellent horse, frightening speed

Rā'id (رَائِض) A breaker or trainer

Rā'iq (رَائِق) Beautiful, comely, attractive

Rā'ish (رَائِش) An agent, a feathered arrow

Rabāb (رَبَاب) White clouds

Rabīb (رَبِيب) Fed, nourished, foster mother, step daughter

Rābid (رَابِضْ) Kneeling down, lying down, resting

Rabīd (رَبِيد) Dates in a jar with water sprinkled upon it.

Rābid (رَابِد) One who repasts, guards property, a woman who alights in a place

Rābigh (رَابِغ) Easy, comfortable

Rābih (رَابِح) Trafficking in one gains

Rabīh (رَبِيح) Trafficking in one gains

Rabīl (رَبِيل) Fleshy and large bodied, silent

Rabīq (رَبِيق) One who has wool upon the head, the cake of a bread

Rabīs (رَبِيس) Courageous, brave

Rabīth (رَبِيث) To be hindered, withheld

Rādib (رَاضِب) Abundant and extensive rain, lote tree

Radīgh (رَدِيغ) Thrown down, prostrated

Radīm (رَدِيم) An old garment

Rādin (رَادِن) Intensely dusky

Rafī' (رَفِيع) High, elevated

Rāfid (رَافِد) Giving a gift, aiding, tributary, one next to the king in station

Rafīf (رَفِيف) Shinning, glistering

Rāfil (رَافِل) A man who drags his skirt, an elegant gait

Raghwān (رَغْوَان) A certain bird, loquacious and loud

voice

Rahamān (رَهَمَان) A bearing, leaning on one side

Rahbar (رَهْبَر) Guide, leader

Rahīd (رَهِيْد) Delicate, tender, soft

Rahīb (رَحِيب) Ample, spacious, wide place

Rahīd (رَحِيض) A washed garment

Rahīn (رَهِين) Pledged, deposited

Rahīs (رَهِيص) Steadfast, determined, lion

Rahwāz (رَهْوَاز) A gentle pace, slow

Rai'ān (رَيْعَان) Blooming, excellent part of anything

Rā'ib (رَاعِب) Free from doubt and confusion

Rā'id (رَائِد) Supple, fresh, tender, goodly

Rā'if (رَائِف) Pitiful, merciful, compassionate

Rā'ih (رَائِح) journeying or working in afternoon

Rā'il (رَائِل) Falling in drops

Rā'im (رَائِم) Very familiar, acquainted, an ewe, goat

Rīmān (رِيْمَان) Inclined, drawn together, excess, abundance

Raimān (رَيْمَان) Inclining, leaning

Rā'iq (رَائِق) Pure, sincere, pleasure, exciting, admiration

Rā'is (رَائِس) A fine camel

Rā'ith (رَائِث) Slow, dilator, tardy, sluggish

Rakīn (رَكِين) A mountain having high sides, difficult of access

Ram'ān (رَمْعَان) Trembling, shaking, to walk fastly

Ramīl (رَمِيْل) Having a little rain or sand, an adorer

Rāmīn (رَامِين) Obedient, humble, thrower of arrows

Ramīd (رَمِيض) Sharp spear,

sharpened, swift

Rāmik (رَامِك) Remaining, staying, abiding

Rāmiq (رَامِق) Remaining, staying, one who has little love

Rāmis (رَامِس) A low and gentle sound, something that flies by night

Rāmish (رَامِشْ) Harmony, melody, having sourness of the eyes

Rāmīsh (رامِيش) Harmony, melody

Rāmith (رَامِث) Slow, tardy, late

Ramīz (رَمِيز) Intelligent, noble, agile, swift

Rammāth (رَمَّاث) The maker of rafts

Rānij (رَانِج) A kind of a smooth date, coconut

Ranīm (رَنِيم) A good, pleasing sound

Rawmān (رَوْمَان) One who is preplanned and confounded

Raqadān (رَقَدَان) Leaping up like a lamb, a kid

Rāqil (رَاقِل) Tall, high

Raqīq (رَقِيق) Soft, tender fine, thin, sensitive heart, a slave

Rasīm (رَسِيم) A certain pace of a camel, gentle pace

Rashād (رَشَاد) Right procedure, holding a right belief

Rashīd (رَشِيد) One who is following the right way

Rāshid (رَاشِد) Taking or following a right way

Rashīq (رَشِيق) Shooting arrows, active, sharp

Rāshiq (رَاشِق) Light and active man, one who shoots arrows

Rāsib (رَاسِب) A firm mountain

Rasīf (رَسِيف) One who walks in short steps

Rāsim (رَاسِم) Running water,

a gentle pace

Rathīd (رَثِيد) The household, goods

Rathīm (رَثِيم) Pebble broken in pieces

Rātib (رَاطِب) Constant and continual, firm

Ratīm (رَتِيم) A slow pace, a thread, string

Rātim (رَاطِم) Keeping, adhering, to a thing

Rātiq (رَاتِق) Clouds closing up

Rawāhah (رَوَاحه) Joy, sprightliness, lively

Rayyān (رَيَّان) Well watered, satisfied, plump

Razān (رَزَان) Chaste, firm, constant

Rāzih (رَازِح) An emancipated or fatigued camel

Razīm (رَزِيم) Roaring, a lion

Rāzim (رَازِم) Firm, steadfast, standing still, motionless, the lion

Razīn (رَزِين) Heavy, weighty, grave, redate, calm, still

Rāzin (رَازِن) Heavy, weighty, steady

Ri'ān (رِعَان) A long mountain, prominent part of a mountain

Ri'ās (رِئَاس) The beginning of an affair

Ri'āth (رِعَاث) Ear-ring

Ribāb (رِبَاب) A fresh state, beginning of anything

Ribāh (رِبَاح) Gain, profit

Rībāl (رِيبَال) The lion

Rib'ī (رِبْعِي) Relating to the spring season, fresh, born in the spring time

Ridāh (رِدَاح) A great bowl

Ridfān (رِدْفَان) Two sailors in the hinder part of the ship

Rihān (رِهَان) A thing deposited as a stake, wager

Risāgh (رِسَاغ) A cord, rope

Ritaq (رِتَاق) A garment

Riwā' (رِوَاء) A rope

Riyāsh (رِيَاش) Superb or excellent clothing

Riyāt (رِيَاط) A kind of woolen cloth

Rizāgh (رِزَاغ) Moisture

Rizām (رِزَام) Strong, stubborn, the lion

Rauqān (رَوْقَان) A resolute and determined

Raushān (رَوْشَان) Stars, well-known

Rudāh (رُدَاح) Big bowl

Rubaidān (رُبَيْدَان) A certain plant

Rubbān (رُبَّان) A profit, the first, beginning state of anything

Ruhāb (رُحَاب) Ample, spacious, wide place

Ruhām (رُهَام) A certain non-preying bird

Rukām (رُكَام) The clouds collected together, a thin accumulated

Rukānah (رُكَانَه) Firmness, gravity, solidity

Rumaih (رُمَيْح) A staff, small lance or spear

Rūmān (رُوْمَان) Middle, romance, affection

Ruwaifi' (رُوَيْفِع) Noble, gentle, exalted, high

Ruwwām (رُوَّام) A seeking one, desiring for

Ru'yān (رُؤْيَان) To see, observe

Ru'yān (رُعْيَان) Rulers, governors

Ruzām (رُزَام) Firm, steadfast

Sa'b (صَعْب) To be difficult, hard

Sabāh (صَبَاح) A lamp lighted wick

Sabhān (صَبْحَان) One who has taken morning draught

Sabīb (صَبِيب) Poured out or forth, honey

Sabīh (صَبِيح) Beautiful, pretty, bright

Sābih (سَابِح) A swimmer, swimming

Sābih (صابح) The plain, manifest

Sabīkh (سَبِيخ) Cotton, wool, soft hair

Sabrah (سَبْرَه) A cold morning, intenseness of the cold of winter

Sadīm (سَدِيم) Haze, mist, remembering (Allah), much mentioned

Saddām (صَدَّام) One who knocks, dashes against, strikes someone

Sadīl (سَدِيل) Cloth cover of a camel litter, curtain

Sādim (سَادِم) Repenting , grieving, anxious

Sadīn (سَدِين) Fat, veil curtain, blood, wool

Sādin (سَادِن) Servant, minister of the Ka'bah

Sadamān (سَدَمَان) Repenting, grieving, anxious

Safdar (صَفْدَر) Courageous, bold

Saffān (سَفَّان) A constructor, maker of ships

Saffār (صَفَّار) A frequent whistler

Safiyy (صَفِيّ) Pure, chosen, sincere friend,

Safwān (صَفْوَان) Soft and smooth stones, bright and clear day

Sahām (سَهَام) Burning, vehement heat of summer, hot winds

Sahbal (سَحْبَل) A large and big bucket

Sahbān (سَحْبَان) A great orator, strong man who carries away everything

Suhbān (سُحبَان) A remaining portion of water in a pool

Sahīm (سَحِيم) A certain plant, clouds

Sahīm (سَهِيم) Protector, companion

Saibān (صَيْبَان) The herbage produced after rain

Sā'id (سَائِد) Prevailing, prevalent, dominant, ruling

Saidān (صَيْدَان) Pieces of silver

Saif (سَيْف) Sword, saber, rapier

Sā'in (صَائِن) Protector, guard, preserver

Sainīm (سَيْنِيم) Raised, exalted

Sajāwal (سَجَاوَل) Adorned, noble friend

Sajīh (سَجِيح) Gentle, even, easy, straight

Sajīl (سَجِيل) A large, big bucket, big bowl

Sajīr (سَجِير) A sincere, true friend, close companion

Salīt (سَلِيط) To be strong, hard, sharp, loquacious

Salīd (صَلِيد) Hard and smooth stone

Salīl (سَلِيل) Descendant, offspring, drawn sword, colt, pure wine, spinal marrow

Samāmah (سَمَامَه) A swift she-camel, swallows, a banner standard

Samayān (صَمَيَان) To hasten, be light, active, agile, befall

Samīd (سَمِيد) white, whitened flour

Sāmid (سَامِد) A man standing or raising his head

Samīh (سَمِيح) Liberal, bountiful, generous

Sāmih (سَامِح) Gentle, excellent in manners

Sāmil (سَامِل) One who strives for right management, canopus, a star

Samīm (صَمِيم) Real, genuine, absolute

Sāmin (سَامِن) Fat, having much flesh, possessor of butter

Samīn (سَمِين) Fat, plump, having much flesh

Sāmiq (سَامِق) High, towering

Sāmir (صَامِر) A day in which wind is still

Sāmit (سَامِط) Boiling water, to hang something behind

Samīt (سَمِيط) A lamb, kid, a roasted sheep

Sammāk (سَمَّاك) Fish monger, fish dealer, fisher

Sammāl (سَمَّال) One who puts out the eyes of others

Simmān (سِمَّان) A certain plant

Sammān (سَمَّان) A seller of butter, certain dyes for embellishment

Sammān (صَمَّان) Rugged or hard ground, rugged place

Sammās (سَمَّاس) A seller of pearls

Samsām (صَمْصَام) A sharp sword

Samsām (سَمْسَام) Light, active and agile, light and slender

Sanān (سَنَان) Spearhead, arrowhead

Sanīh (سَنِيح) Large pearls

Sannān (صَنَّان) Core, innermost, courageous, brave

Saqrān (صَقْرَان) Dates moistened with milk, butter

Sarfān (صَرْفَان) Day and night

Sarfarāz (سَرْفَرَاز) High, exalted, lofty

Sārif (صَارِف) To make a grating or creaking sound

Sawīd (سويد) A chief lord, master

Sawwām (صَوَّام) A man who fasts often

Sawwār (سَوَّار) Enthusiastic, one who is ready to leap or spring upon, lion

Sayām (سَيَام) A sort of bird

Sayyūr (صَيُّور) End, last of anything, bright opinion

Shā'il (شَائِل) Active and clever, swift, a fine camel

Shāhīn (شَاهِين) Falcon, peregrine

Shabbīr (شَبِّير) Pious, beautiful, handsome

Shabī' (شَبِيع) A piece of garment, food, satiated

Shabīb (شَبِيب) Young man, youth

Shādhib (شَاذِب) Foreigner, stranger, solitary, alone

Shādin (شَادِن) A young gazelle, fawn

Shafīq (شَفِيق) Compassionate, tender, fearful, anxious

Shahbāz (شَهْبَاز) A royal falcon, generous, noble

Shahīr (شَهِير) Celebrated, noted eminent, generally known

Shāh Jahān (شَاهْ جَهَان) King of the world

Shāh Nawāz (شَاه نَوَاز) One who grants the kings

Shahraiz (شَهْرِيز) Dated

Shāhrukh (شَاهْ رُخ) Extensively handsome, beautiful

Shahwār (شَهْوَار) Princely, worthy of a king

Shahzaib (شَهْزِيب) Royal beauty

Shahm (شَهْم) To protect, guard, bold

Shā'iq (شَائِق) Exciting desire, desirable, admiring lover

Shajī' (شَجِيع) Courageous, valiant, bold

Shakīb (شَكِيب) Patient, enduring

Shakīl (شَكِيل) Handsome, well shaped, comely

Shamā'il (شَمَائِل) Merit, good feature, character, nature

Shāmikh (شَامِخ) High, elevated, lofty, proud

Shāmil (شَامِل) Comprehensive, exhaustive, extensive, general

Shāmis (شَامِس) Sunny, sunshine day, clear

Shamīt (شَمِيط) Mixed together

Shamshīr (شَمْشِير) A sword

Shaqrān (شَقْرَان) Having a fair and ruddy complexion

Sha'rān (شَعْرَان) A place abounding with trees

Shārib (شَارِب) Drinking, a drinker

Shārid (شَارِد) Taking a flight, fleeing away

Sharīf (شَرِيف) Noble, of noble lineage, eminent

Shārif (شَارِف) High and advanced in age

Sharīs (شَرِيس) A bold, daring in fight

Shāriz (شَارِز) One who has a fork

Shurahbīl (شُرَحْبِيل) The name of a Prophet's companion ﷺ

Shaukat (شَوْكَت) Grandeur, great strength or valour

Shāzib (شَازِب) To be lean, light of flesh, lank, slender, rough

Shamīr (شَمِيْر) Clever, skilful, to exert ones self vigorously

Shair Afgan (شِيرافْگَن) One who overthrows or hurls a lion

Shehryār (شَهْرِيَار) A despotic ruler, a king, a prince

Shimās (شِمَاس) A horse that refuses to be ridden

Shimmīr (شِمِّير) One who strives, labors or exerts

Shakhīs (شَخِيص) A lord, master, man of rank and quality

Shamrīz (شَمْرِيز) Filled up to nails

Shubrumah (شُبْرُمَه) Gift, present

Shujā' (شُجَاع) Courageous, brave, bold

Shujā'at (شُجَاعت) Courage, bravery, boldness

Sibdān (سِبْدَان) A piece of cloth

Sifād (صِفَاد) A rope, fetter, shackle

Sijāh (سِجَاح) The air, beauty, exactness, justness of proportion

Sildam (صِلْدَام) Hard and smooth, tough

Sīmāb (سِيمَاب) Mercury, quick silver

Simād (صِمَاد) Stopper, a kerchief, a piece of cloth

Simāl (سِمَال) The remaining water at the watering trough

Simān (سمان) Plump, fat

Simmān (سِمَّان) The decoration, embellishment

Simt (سِمْط) A thread, string having upon it beads

Sinād (سِنَاد) Strong

Sināk (صِنَاك) Hard and strong, bulky, big bodied

Sinān (سِنَان) A spearhead, the spear

Sindān (سِنْدَان) Great and strongman, brave

Sindar (سِنْدَر) Bold, daring, courageous

Sirān (صِيرَان) A sweet odor, root of a palm-tree

Sirdan (صِرْدَان) White place or fur on the hump of a camel

Siyār (صِيَار) A small quantity of musk

Sudaim (سُدَيْم) Remembering Allah, celebrating, much mentioned

Sufyān (سُفْيَان) Intense wind

Suhaib (صُهَيْب) Having redness in the hair

Suhmān (سُهْمَان) A companion, intimate friend

Suhbān (صُحْبَان) A lot, share, portion

Sujāh (سُجَاح) The air, beauty, exactness of proportion

Sumair (صُمَير) The time of sunset

Sumlān (سُمْلاَن) Remains of the beverage

Suwaid (سُوَيْد) Quite early in the morning

Tābish (تَابِش) Refulgence, brilliance, splendor, heat, grief

Tahseen (تَحْسِيْن) Embellishment, adornment, approval

Taimūr (تَيْمُوْر) Strong, firm, iron, brave

Tajammul (تَجَمُّل) To be embellished, to bear poverty with patience

Tallāl (طَلاَّل) Beautiful, beauty of color, brightness

Tāmir (تَامِر) One who possesses dried dates

Tārim (طَارِم) Dome, high, exalted

Tasawwur (تَصَوُّر) Imagination, conception

Thabīn (ثَبِين) Extremity or border of the garment

Tha'd (ثَعْد) Soft, tender, fresh, juicy

Thāghim (ثَاغِم) White color

Thā'ib (ثَائِب) A violent wind that blows at the beginning of rain

Thumāl (ثُمَال) An aider, succorer, any kind of milk when it is drawn

Thumāmah (ثُمَامَه) Panicum grass

Thāmid (ثَامِد) A calf that begins to eat

Thamīl (ثَمِيل) A little water

Thāmir (ثَامِر) Perfect, complete, respect of forbearance

Thaqīf (ثَقِيف) Sharp, skilful, active, penetrating

Tharwān (ثَرْوَان) A bounding in cattle or other property

Tharwat (ثَرْوَت) Plenty, abundance, wealth, riches

Thibān (ثِبَان) Border of a garment, receptacle

Thimād (ثِمَاد) A little quantity of water, a well

Thimāl (ثِمَال) Froth of any kind

Thubān (ثُبان) A receptacle

Tufail (طُفَيْل) Any part or portion of a thing

Ubayy (أُبَيْ) Proudy, one who disdains to do a base thing

'Ubdān (عُبْدَان) Tall palm-trees

'Ukkāshah (عُكَّاشَه) Spider, spider web

'Ulwan (عُلْوَان) A book of writing

'Uqbān (عُقْبَان) The end, last of anything

'Urbān (عُرْبَان) An earnest and pure money, raceme of a palm-tree, dates

'Urmān (عُرْمَان) The places of seed produce, cultivators of land

'Urs (عُرْس) Wedding ceremony, bridal

'Urshān (عُرْشَان) Two ears, two veins in the base of the neck

'Urwah (عُرْوَه) A button loop, handle, a thing by which another thing is rendered firm and fast

Usāmah (اُسَامَه) Lion, courageous

Usaid (اُسَيْد) Small lion

'Ushbān (عُشْبَان) A palm-branch, white skin

'Utās (عُطَاس) The dawn, daybreak

Uthāl (اُثَال) Glorified, dignified

'Uthmān (عُثْمَان) A young bustard

Wabbās (وَبَّاص) Intense light, illuminated, bright

Wabīs (وَبِيص) Shining, gleaming, bright

Wābis (وَابِص) Shining, gleaming, glistening

Wābisah (وَابِصَه) Flash, lightning, brilliant

Wabsān (وَبْصَان) Bright, shining, illuminated

Wadī' (وَدِيْع) Quiet, gentle, peaceable

Wadīn (وَضِين) A girth wide woven of hair, skin

Wafīq (وَفِيق) Companion, friend

Wa'īb (وَعِيْب) The mainstay or supply, support of another

Wā'il (وَائِل) Deliverance, salvation, liberation

Wajāhat (وَجَاهَت) High esteemed, to be respected, glory

Wajīd (وَجِيد) Smooth land, plain

Wazīn (وَزِين) A prudent, reflecting person

Wajīn (وَجِين) Border of a valley, rough and hard ground

Wakīf (وَكِيف) Rain, to drop, trickle water

Waqār (وَقَار) Gravity, steadiness, calmness

Waqās (وَقَاص) Excellent warrior, fighter

Waqīd (وَقِيد) Fuel, anything to kindle a fire

Waqīr (وَقِير) Heavily burdened with debt

Waqqād (وَقَّاد) Clever, sharp ardent, fiery

Wārid (وَارِد) Arriving, new comer, possible

Wāshij (وَاشِج) The hardest of canes

Wāshiz (وَاشِظ) Anything entangled, intermixed

Washīz (وَشِيظ) Follower, ally, attendant

Wasīf (وَصِيْف) Young servant, butler, valet

Wasīl (وَصِيل) An intimate companion, friend

Wasīm (وَسِيم) Handsome, pretty, candy

Wasīq (وَسِيق) Rain

Wasīt (وَسِيط) Mediator, agent, middle

Warqah (وَرْقَه) A leaf, paper, slip

Wāthīj (وَاثِج) Dense, thick herbage

Wathij (وَثِيج) Dense and thick herbage

Wāthilah (وَاثِلَه) Rope of palm fibers or of camel-hamp

Wathīr (وَثِير) Plain, smooth, soft, easy

Wazīf (وَظِيف) The slender part of the shank

Wirshān (وِرْشَان) One who hides his origin

Wisām (وِسَام) Beautiful, handsome

Withār (وِثَار) Plainness, softness, smoothness

Yāfi' (يَافِع) Adolescent, grown up, juvenile, teenager

Yamān (يَمَان) Blessed, on the right side

Ya'sūb (يَعْسُوب) Drone, male bee, chief, title of Ali ﷺ

Yāwar (يَاوَر) Aiding, an assistant, companion, friendly

Zabīb (زَبِيب) Raisins, dried fruit, currants, dried figs

Zābid (زَابِد) Possessor of fresh butter

Zabīl (زَبِيل) A basket of palm-leaves

Zābil (زَابِل) A short man

Zābin (زَابِن) Brave, perfect soldiers, the prefect

Zabīn (زَبِين) One who is strong, pushing

Zabīr (زَبِير) A strong, skilful and ingenious man

Zafar (زَفَر) A large gift, liberal man, a river

Zafīf (زَفِيف) To make haste, quick and violent mind

Zāfir (زَافِر) One who helps to carry loads, a group or army

Zaghīd (زَغِيد) Fresh butter

Zaib (زيب) Elegance, adorning, brisk, lively

Zalīj (زَلِيج) Quick and swift camel

Zālij (زَالِج) Quick and swift

Zalkhān (زَلْخَان) The advancing, quick

Zamān (زَمَان) Time, epoch, age, period

Zamīr (زَمِير) A short man

Zamī‘ (زَمِيع) A sharp, vigorous, courageous man

Zimā‘ (زِمَاع) A man strong, vigorous and sharp

Zamīl (زَمِيل) A traveling companion, one who rides behind another

Zarārah (زَرَارَه) Intelligent, sharp, skilful

Zarīr (زَرِير) Light, active, sagacious, skill

Zarīm (زَرِيم) One who does not remain fixed

Zarnab (زَرْنَب) A certain sweet smelling tree, perfume

Zarnāb (زَرْنَاب) Pure gold

Zarrār (زَرَّار) Sharp, intelligent, skilled, light

Zaryāb (زَرْيَاب) Wealthy, rich

Zayyān (ظَيَّان) Honey, wild jasmine

Zīrak (زِيرَك) Wise, intelligent, shrewd

Zibāl (زِبَال) A minor thing

Zinbīl (زِنْبِيل) A basket of palm leaves

Ziryāb (زِرْيَاب) Gold, water-gold

Ziyān (زِيَان) Decoration, ornament, beautifying

Zarīf (ظَرِيف) Beautiful, elegant, witty, humorous, cute

Zu’āf (زُؤَاف) Quick in effect

Zu’aib (زُؤَيْب) One who drinks a little

Zubāb (زُبَاب) Dried figs, rainsins, dried grapes

Zubaid (زُبَيْد) Chosen, selected

Zubair (زُبَيْر) Powerful man, acute, sharp clever

Zublān (زُبْلاَن) Palm, leaf-baskets

Zum‘ah (زُمْعَه) The fortress of grass

Zunnār (زُنَّار) A waist belt

‘Ātikah (عَاتِكَه) Red, pure yellow, an old bow

Islamic Names for the Muslim Females

'Ātiqah (عَاتِقَه) An excellent, generous woman, old bow

'Abālah (عَبالَه) The mountain rose

'Abīlah (عَبِيلَه) A bulky and strong woman

'Abīrah (عَبِيرَه) A certain mixture of perfume

Ābrū (آبْرُو) Honor, prestige, character, fame

'Ābyah (عابِيَه) A beautiful woman

Adā (ادَا) Expression, elegance, grace, execution

Adhkiyah (اَذْكِيَه) Sagacious, sharp witted

'Afīfah (عَفِيفَه) Pure, chaste, virtuous

'Afīrah (عَفِيرَه) Dust colored, white

'Afrā' (عَفْرَاء) Dustcolored, white

Afshān (اَفْشَان) To sprinkle, tinsel, strips

Afshīn (اَفْشِين) Golden

Afzā (افْزَا) Adding, augmenting

Ā'ibah (آئِبَه) To come to water, draught

'Ā'idah (عَائِدَه) Favor, kindness, compassion, to repeat, coming back

'Aidānah (عَيْدَانَه) A tall tree

Ā'ilah (آئِلَه) Exquisitely handsome, beautiful

'Ā'imah (عَائِمَه) Tedious, severe years, ships, swimmer

Ā'imah (آئِمَه) The exemplar, head, road, strong

Aimal (اَيْمَل) Desire, hope, expecting

Aiman (اَيْمَن) The right, dexter

Aimah (عَيْمَة) The desire, longing for milk

Ā'irah (آئِرَه) Noble, glorified, honorable

Ā'irīn (آئِرِين) Reconciliation, peace

'Aitā' (عَيْطَا) Long in the neck

'Aithah (عَيْثَه) A plain, soft tract of land

A'izzah (اَعِزَّه) Stranger, noble, dear

Ajyah (اَجْيَه) Excellent, noble

Ālifah (آلِفَه) To be familiar with, accustomed to

Alīfāh (اَلِيفَه) Sociable, friendly, companionable

'Alīnah (عَلِينَه) Manifest

'Alīthah (عَلِيثَه) Wheat mixed with barley

'Alīzah (عَلِيزَه) Anxious, one who is inclined

Al-khansā' (اَلْخَنْسَاء) A gazelle, wild cow

Almīrah (اَلْمِيرَه) A princess

Alwīnah (اَلْوِينَه) Pretty, handsome, lovely

Alwiyah (اَلْوِيَه) A banner, standard, thin sand

Ambar (اَمْبَر) Sky, clouds, covering

Ambarīn (اَمْبَرِين) Sky, covering

'Ambarīn (عَنْبَرِين) Emitting the smell of ambergris

'Amīmah (عَمِيمَه) Tall, perfect in stature

Amīrah (اَمِيرَه) Chieftess, princess

Āmirah (آمِرَه) To command, spell enjoin upon

Anasah (اَنَسَه) To be polite, affable, sociable

'Anbar (عَنْبَر) Ambergris store-house

'Anbasah (عَنْبَسَه) Lioness, brave, courageous

'Anbīzah (عَنْبِيزه) Isolated, alone

'Anbrīnah (عَنْبَرِينه) Sweet like ambergris

'Andalīb (عَنْدَلِيب) Nightingale

Anīlā (اَنِيلَا) Inexperienced, naive, imprudent

Anzīlah (انزيلَه) Alighting, descending

Anīqah (اَنِيقَه) A meadow, beautiful garden, unique

Ānisah (آنِسَه) Polite, affable, friendly

Āniyah (آنِيَه) A vessel, a receptacle of water, hot

Anjashah (اَنْجَشَه) One who spreads a news

Anūshah (اَنُوْشَه) Glad, cheerful

'Anwah (عَنْوَه) Humble, lowly, obedient, submissive

'Anzah (عَنْزَه) A short spear Javelin

'Aqīsah (عَقِيصَه) Twisted lock of a woman

'Aqsā' (عَقْصا) A woman who has twisted locks

Artāshah (اَرْتَاشَه) To rectify or amend a condition

Arāthah (اَرَاثَه) The means of kindling

'Arbā (عَرْبَا) Pure and chaste in speech

Arībah (اَرِيبَه) Skilful, sagacious, intelligent, sly

Arīdah (اَرِيضَه) Productive, pleasing to the eye, thriving land

Arīhah (اَرِيحَه) To give rest, to ease

Arīj (اَرِيج) Fragrance, scent, perfume

Arījah (اَرِيجَه) A sweet odor, to exhale odor

Arīkah (اَرِيكَه) A raised couch

'Arīqah (عَرِيقَه) Noble, high esteemed, exalted

Armān (اَرْمَان) Desire, longing, yearning

Armā (اَرْمَا) Strong, fortified

Armīn (اَرْمِين) Fortified

'Arūb (عَرُوْب) Showing great love or fondness

'Arūbah (عَرُوبَه) An ancient name of Friday, chaste in speech

'Arūbiyyah (عُرُوْبِيَّه) Eloquent, pure in speech

Arwā (اَرْوي) To water, irrigate plentifully

Ārzū (آرْزُو) Wish, desire, longing

'Asbah (عَسْبَه) A cleft, fissure in a mountain

'Ashbah (عَشْبَه) Fresh, green, soft herbage

'Ashībah (عَشِيبَه) A country, a place of meadows

'Āshibah (عَاشِبَه) A country land producing herbs

Āsifah (آصِفَه) Intelligent, sagacious

Āsirah (آصِرَه) A small rope, a tie of kindred

Āsiyā (آسِيَا) A mill, grinding mill

Āsiyah (آسِيَه) Pillar, column, strong or fortified building

Asmā (اَصْمي) To be light, active, to leap or hasten

Asmārah (اَسْمارَه) Brownish, dusky, tarnish

Athīlah (اَثِيْلَه) Glory, dignity, high rank

'Atīf (عَطِيف) Gentle, very submissive, humble

'Ātikah (عَاتِكَه) An old red bow, perfumed

'Atīqah (عَتِيقَه) A beautiful woman, generous, excellent

Bādhikhah (بَاذِخَه) High, elevated mountain, prominent

Bādhilah (بَاذِلَه) Generous, liberal

Bādi'ah (بَادِئَه) The start of anything, to begin something

Badīhah (بَدِيهَه) The first occurrence of anything

Bādihah (بَادِهَه) To come upon someone suddenly

Badīlah (بَدِيلَه) Substitute, replacement, spare

Bādilah (بَادِلَه) Brocade, gold or silver thread

Bādinah (بَادِنه) Heavy by reason of age, big bodied

Bādirah (بَادِرَه) Hastiness of temper, passionate

Badrah (بَدْرَه) Quick sighted, round and large, hastiness, passionate

Bahjat (بَهْجَت) Gladness, splendour, joy

Bājisah (بَاجِسَه) Flowing water

Bakhtāwar (بَخْتَاوَر) Lucky, fortunate

Bakīrah (بَكِيرَه) First fruit, a palm tree

Bāniyah (بَانِيَه) Builder, founder

Barī'ah (بَرِيعَه) A woman excelling in goodness, beauty or intelligence

Bāri'ah (بَارِعَه) A beautiful, goodly girl

Barīdah (بَرِيدَه) Freshness, coolness

Bāriqah (بَارِقَه) A lightening cloud, swords

Barīrah (بَرِيرَه) Pious

Barqa' (بَرْقَا) Having black and white colors

Bārrah (بَارَّه) Gentle, good and affectionate to others, true oath

Bashārah (بَشَارَه) Goodness, elegance of form and feature

Bashnīn (بَشْنِين) Blue lotus

Bāsiqah (بَاسِقَه) Exceedingly tall palm-tree

Bāsirah (بَاصِرَه) Knowledge, intelligence, perception, skill

Basīrah (بَصِيرَه) Perception, sagacity, wisdom, skill

Basītah (بَسِيطَه) A wide, spacious place

Bāsitah (بَاسِطَه) To act boldly, freely, cheerfully

Bāthiqah (بَاثِقه) A well full of water

Bathnā' (بَثناء) A plain and smooth land

Batīlah (بَتِيلَه) Any limb with its flesh, virgin

Batūl (بَتُوْل) Elegant, virgin, a limb, a shoot

Bāzilā (بَازِلَا) Green pea (A plant)

Bilqīs (بِلْقِيس) Beautiful, the queen of Saba

Bīnish (بِينِش) Discernment, eye sight

Bithnah (بِثْنَه) A smooth, plain ground

Dabā'ah (ضَبَاعَه) Fast, speedy

Dafīrah (ضَفِيرَه) A plaited lock of hair

Dāfirah (ضَافِرَه) Helper, supporter, assistant

Dā'isah (دَائِصَه) One who follows the magistrate

Dājinah (دَاجِنَه) A cloud raining continuously

Dalsā' (دَلْصَاء) Very smooth, soft land

Damāmah (دَمَامَه) Sagacity, sense, repulsed

Dāman (دَامَن) Skiff (of garment), foot (of a hill)

Damīdah (دَمِيدَه) To sprout, attack, blow

Damīrah (ضَمِيرَه) A lock, plaited lock of hair

Dāmirah (ضَامِره) Lean, slender

Damīthah (دَمِيثَه) Generous, soft, easy nature

Dāmiyah (دَامِيَه) Hunter

Darakhshān (دَرَخْشَان) Shining, luminous, brilliant

Darakhshandah (دَرَخْشَنْدَه) Bright, luminous

Dardā' (دَرْدَاء) A toothless woman

Dau 'Afshan (ضَوْافْشَان) Brilliant, illuminant, bright

Dhakāwat (ذَكَاوَت) Brightness, brilliant,

intelligence

Dhakiyyah (ذَكِيَّه) Sharp witted, bright, intelligent

Dhāmilah (ذَامِله) She-camel that goes at a gentle pace

Dhamīlah (ذَمِيلَه) She camel that walks at a gentle pace

Dhihbah (ذِهْبَه) A copious or light rain

Dhuhaibah (ذُهَيْبَه) A little piece of gold

Dībā (دِيْبَا) Silkbrocade, silk cloth

Dibājah (دِيبَاجَه) A preface to a book composed in an ornate style

Dimādah (ضِمَادَه) Verge, edge of anything

Dīmah (دِيْمَه) A lasting rain

Dimāmah (ضِمَامَه) The two sides of the book

Dumyah (دُمْيَه) A statue, figure, image

Durr Afshān (دُرافْشَان) One who spreads or scatters pearls

Durr-e-Shahwar (دُرِّشَهْوَار) A royal pearl

Durānah (دُرَانَه) Broken in pieces

Durdānah (دُرْدَانَه) A pearl

Durrah (دُرَّه) A large pearl

Durrāj (دُرَّاج) Francolin, healthy cock

Durr-e-Thamīn (دُرِّثَمِين) Costly pearl

Fādirah (فَادِرَه) A portion of the night

Fāghirah (فَاغِرَه) A certain perfume, the roots of the lotus tree

Fahīmah (فَهِيمَه) Intelligent, having much understanding

Fahīrah (فَهِيرَه) Pure, unmixed

Fahmīdah (فَهْمِيدَه) Wise, sagacious

Fā'idah (فَائِدَه) Benefit, profit, interest

Fā'ijah (فَائِجَه) A wide tract between two elevated portions

Fā'imah (فَائِمَه) Watered, filled with herbage

Fāi'yah (فَائِيَه) An elevated and expanded place

Falāhah (فَلاَحَه) Successful, a farmer

Falīhah (فَلِيحَه) Pericarp of the tree

Fāmiyā (فَامِيَا) The seller of fruit, well reputed

Far'ā' (فَرْعَاء) A woman having much hair

Far'ah (فَرْعَه) Elevated place, top (of a mountain)

Farāhah (فَرَاهَه) Beauty, comeliness

Farāsat (فَرَاسَت) Sagacity, shrewdness, discernment

Farhā' (فَرْهَآء) Beautiful, rejoicing

Farhah (فَرْحَه) A joy, gladness, happiness

Farhānah (فَرْحَانَه) Glad, rejoicing, happy

Farī'ah (فَرِيعَه) Excellent, unique, high bough

Fāri'ah (فَارِعَه) High, overtopping, fine lodging

Farīdah (فَرِيدَه) Highly esteemed, precious

Fārizah (فَارِزَه) A species of ants

Farzīn(فَرْزِين) Exalted, high, distinguished

Farkhandah (فَرْخَنْدَه) Auspicious, lucky, fortunate

Farwah (فَرْوَه) A furred garment, the scalp or skin of the head

Farzah (فَرْزَه) A cleft in rugged ground, a piece of detached portion

Farzānah (فَرْزَانَه) Wise, rational, wisdom

Farzīn (فَرْزِين) Queen, wise

Fatāhah (فَتَاحَه) Help

Fātimah (فَاطِمَه) Suckling, weaning, rescued from the Hell-fire

Fātishah (فَاتِشَه) To examine,

inquire diligently

Fazārah (فَزارَه) A wide conspicuous road

Fāzirah (فَازِرَه) A soft wide and compact road

Fidrah (فِدْرَه) A place in a mountain, piece of flesh

Fihāmah (فِهامَه) To comprehend, understand

Fihrah (فِهْرَه) Pure, unmixed

Fildhah (فِلْذَه) Metal, a piece of gold, silver, flesh, meat

Findīrah (فِنْدِيرَه) A piece of mountain

Fitāhah (فِتَاحَه) The office of a judge

Fushah (فُسْحَه) Spaciousness, roominess, width

Furdah (فُرضَه) A hole, a gap in a wall

Furhah (فُرْهَه) A beautiful and comely girl

Furūhah (فُرُوهَه) Skilfulness

Ghādah (غَادَه) Delicate, soft tender

Ghadīrah (غَدِيرَه) A plaited lock of hair

Ghāliyah (غَالِيَه) A certain compound of perfumes

Ghāniyah (غَانِيَه) A young beautiful woman, chaste

Ghazal (غَزَل) Amatory talk and action or poetry

Ghazālah (غَزَالَه) Female gazelle, fawn, warming in the sun

Ghazīlah (غَزِيلَه) Young gazelle, abundance

Ghāziyah (غَازِيَه) A company of fighters

Ghidfah (غِدْفَه) The apparel of the king

Ghunwah (غُنوَه) Freedom from need, competence, richness

Gul (گُل) A rose flower, ornament, brand the mark

Gul Afshān (گُل افشان) Scattering rose,

Gul Ārā (گُل آرا) One who adorns with flowers

Gul Badan (گُل بَدَن) Delicate, graceful, having rose like soft body

Gul Nār (گُل نَار) Pomegranate, flower, rivulet, color

Gul Nāz (گُل نَاز) A beautiful flower

Gul Raiz (گُل ریز) Shedding flower, a kind of fine work

Gul Ra'nā (گُل رعنا) A beautiful delicate, scented rose

Gul Rukh (گُل رخ) Rosy cheeked

Hidhfah (حِذْفَه) Style, a piece of garment

Hādhibah (حَاذِبَه) One who contends in drawing, stretching

Hadīrah (حَضِيرَه) Company, meeting place

Hādirah (حَادِرَه) Goodly, beautiful, fat

Hadrah (حَدْرَه) A single thread

Hāfirah (حَافِرَه) To dig earth, a digger

Hafsah (حَفْصَه) Lioness, name of one of the wives of the Prophet ﷺ

Hājibah (حَاجِبَه) Door keeper, attendant

Hālah (هَالَه) Halo

Hamāmah (حَمَامَه) Pigeon, a handsome woman, dove

Hamdah (هَمْدَه) A trance, apoplexy, calm

Hamdah (حَمْضَه) Eager desire for a thing

Hamīmah (هَمِيمَه) Fine rain, more serious, more important

Hamīzah (حَمِيزَه) Wise, clever, intelligent

Hamnah (حَمْنَه) A sort of grape

Hamsā' (حَمْسَاء) Vehement courage, strong, bold

Hamshā' (حَمْشَاء) Slender in

make, shanks

Hānam (هَانَم) A venerable woman

Hanānah (حَنَانَه) Merciful, moved with compassion

Hānī (هَانِي) A servant, happy, delighted, blessed

Hāniyah (حَانِيَه) Delighted, pleased

Haniyyah (حَنِيَّه) Affection, compassion

Hanā'ah (هَنَآئه) Wine, to rejoice, be happy

Hanwah (حَنْوَه) A plant of sweet odor

Harīm (حَرِيم) Apartment of the women, women of household

Harīrah (حَرِيرَه) A kind of soup

Harīsah (حَرِيصَه) A cloud, vehemently falling rain

Harīthah (حَرِيثَه) Recompense, reward

Harīzah (حَرِيْزَه) Fortified, guarded, valued

Harmalah (حَرْمَلَه) A kind of a garment

Hasānah (حَصَانَه) Impregnable, strong by nature

Hāsinah (حَاصِنَه) Abstaining from what is unlawful, chaste

Hasnā' (حَصْنَاء) Chaste, abstaining from what is unlawful, virtuous

Hawwā' (حَوَّاء) Eve, mother of mankind

Hidānah (هِدَانَه) Reconciliation, truce

Hidhwah (حِذْوَه) A gift, piece of flesh

Hinā (حِنَا) Henna, myrtle

Hind (هِنْد) Name of a female companion of the Prophet ﷺ, a group

Hirā' (حِرَآء) A cave near Makkah

Hirā (حِرَا) Lawn, courtyard

Hizzah (هِزَّه) Briskness,

sprightliness, cheerfulness

Hudhāfah (حُذَافه) Facility, name of the daughter of Halīmah Sa‘diyah

Hudnah (هُدْنه) Reconciliation, truce

Hudrah (حُدْرَه) A herd of camels

Humā (هُمَا) Phoenix, a fabulous bird supposed lucky to come under its shadow

Humsah (حُمْسَه) Honor, courageous

Hunaidah (هُنَيْدَه) A hundred years, a small group

Husālah (حُسَالَه) Remainder of anything,

Husālah (حُصَالَه) What remains of the grain

Husāmah (حُسَامَه) Sharp sword, blade

Husbānah (حُسْبَانَه) Cloud, thunderbolt

‘Iffat (عِفَّت) Abstinence from unlawful things, chaste

Ifrāh (اِفْرَاح) To gladden, delight

Inālah (اِنَالَه) The act of giving, gifting

Ināqah (اِنَاقَه) To have goodliness, beauty, pleasure

‘Inās (عِنَاس) Mirror, advanced in age

’Īnāsā’ (اِينَاسَا) To entertain pleasantly

‘Iqsah (عِقْصَه) Twisted lock of a woman

Iram (اِرَم) Sign, cairn Paradise

Irāthah (اِرَاثَه) Means of kindling or inflaming

‘Isjah (عِسْجَه) A portion of the night

‘Itrah (عِتْرَه) The stem, stock or branches of a tree

Jabālah (جَبَالَه) Tall structured, elevated, lofty

Jabīlah (جَبِيلَه) Nature, original, temperament

Jabīrah (جَبِيرَه) Splints,

bandage

Jablah (جَبْلَه) The origin, the fundamental nature

Jadhbiyah (جَذْبِيَه) Attraction, pulling, drag

Jādhibah (جَاذِبَه) Attraction, allurement, gravity

Jadhlah (جَذْلَه) Joyful, glad, happy

Jā'ibah (جَائِبَه) A thing that traverses the earth from country to country

Jā'ishah (جَائِشَه) Soul, one self, strength of heart

Jalīhah (جَلِيحَه) Hard, eating much

Jalīrah (جَلِيرَه) Strong, healthy, clever

Jamīmah (جَمِيمَه) Lucky, dove

Jammamah (جَمَّامَه) Satiated, full measure

Jarīrah (جَرِيرَه) An earthen vessel

Jāshirah (جَاشِرَه) Free, liver, to let loose the animals

Jazālah (جَزَالَه) Eloquence, abundance, large

Jazīlah (جَزِيلَه) Great, large, intelligent, elegant

Jāzimah (جَازِمَه) Absolute, decided

Jazlā' (جَزْلَاء) Sound, correct, generous

Jāziyah (جَازِيَه) A satisfaction, good for good

Jazlah (جَزْلَه) Sound, correct, generous

Jaibah (جَيْبَه) Answer, reply, response

Judhāmah (جُذَامَه) Mown meadow

Juhānah (جُهَانَه) A young woman

Julaidah (جُلَيْدَه) One of the coats of the eye

Jumānah (جُمَانَه) Beads made of silver

Juwairiyah (جُوَيْرِيه) Wife of the Prophet ﷺ, merrymaker

Kabshah (كَبْشَه) Chief, leader, ram

Kahkashān (كَهْكَشَان) Galaxy, milky way

Kānifah (كَانِفَه) Shelter

Kanwal (كَنْوَل) The lotus, heart

Kashmālah (كَشْمَالَه) A handful, gang, hook, eye

Kathbā' (كَثْبَاء) Earth, soil

Kathbah (كَثْبَه) A little valley, depression

Kaumal (كَوْمَل) Soft, tender, downy, mild, sweet

Khabīrah (خَبِيرَه) Soft wool, an invitation to Aqīqah

Khādibah (خاضِبَه) An ostrich, one who dyes his hair with henna

Khadījah (خَدِيجَه) Imperfect

Khādirah (خَاضِرَه) A palm tree

Khāli'ah (خَالِعَه) Ripe, ready

Khalīsah (خَلِيسَه) Brave, courageous

Khamīsah (خَمِيصَه) A garment

Khamtah (خَمْطَه) A land of fine environment

Khamrah (خَمْرَه) A sweet odor, odor of a perfume, a hiding

Khānam (خَانَم) Princess, lady

Khansā (خَنْسَا) Gazelles, bulls

Khashbah (خَشْبَه) The first filing of a sword

Khashībah (خَشِيبَه) The natural quality of a sword

Khaulah (خَوْلَه) A female gazelle

Khamīlah (خَمِيلَه) Dense trees, thicket, wood

Khizāmah (خِزَامَه) A ring of hair

Khubnah (خُبْنَه) A garment to conceal and carry things

Khush Bakht (خُوشْ بَخت) Lucky

Khuzrah (خُزْرَه) One who

looks from the outer angles of the eyes

Kifāyah (كِفايه) Sufficiency, affluence

Kināfah (كِنافَه) Pastry with sugar and nuts

Kināz (كِناز) Fatty, healthy

Kindah (كِنْدَه) A portion of a mountain

Kiran (كِرَن) Ray, beam, gold or silver

Kishwar (كِشْوَر) A country, climate, region

Kulthūm (كُلْثُوم) A beautiful and attractive face

Kunthah (كُنْثَه) A place for the arrangement of sweet plants

Kunwah (كُنْوَه) Epithet, surname

Labīkah (لَبِيْكَه) A mixture of oil, butter and dates

Labīqah (لَبِيْقَه) Skilful, clever, elegant, fitting

Ladānah (لَدانَه) Flexibility, pliancy, suppleness

Lafītah (لَفِيتَه) A certain thicker kind of food

Lahhāsah (لَحّاسَه) Lioness

Lā'ibah (لَائِبَه) Thirsty

Lālah Rukh (لَالَه رُخ) Rosy cheeked

Lāmiyah (لَامِيَه) A woman having locks

Libābah (لِبَابَه) A kind of garment

Libdah (لِبْدَه) Compact matted wool

Libwah (لِبْوَه) Lioness

Lidah (لِدَه) Of the same age, intimate friend

Līnah (لِينَه) Soft, delicate, flexible, tender

Lubānah (لُبَانَه) Desire, object

Luhbah (لُهْبَه) The whiteness, brightness of the skin

Mādhiyah (مَاذِيَه) White armour

Madhyah (مَذْيَه) Clean mirror, blade

Madīhah (مَدِيحَه)
Praiseworthy, eulogized

Mādihah (مَادِحَه) Eulogist, praiser

Mudiyyah (مُدِيَّه) Distance, extent, a large knife

Madrā' (مَدْرَاء) A city, village, town

Madrah (مَدْرَه) A city, village, town

Mah Jabīn (مَهْ جَبِين)
Exquisitely beautiful, having forehead like a moon

Māhā (مَاهَا) Just like a moon, beautiful

Māhah (مَاحَه) A courtyard in a house

Māham (مَاهَم) My moon, sweet-heart

Mahīn (مَهِين) Fine and thin, feeble, old

Māhīn (مَاهِين) Bright and beautiful like moon

Māhiyyah (مَاهِيَّه) The essence or substance of a thing

Māh Jabīn (مَاهْ جَبِيْن)
Exquisitely beautiful, beloved

Māh Mubīn (مَاهْ مُبِين) Bright, brilliant moon

Māh Pārah (مَاهْ پَارَه)
Handsome, brilliant, beloved

Mahrīn (مَهْرِين) Bright like the sun and moon, beloved

Māh Rukh (مَاهْ رُخ)
Exquisitely beautiful, having a face like the moon

Mahwish (مَهْوِش) Bright, beautiful like the moon

Mai'ah (مَيْعَه) The liveliness, briskness, sprightliness

Mā'ilah (مَائِلَه) Inclined, interested

Maithā' (مَيْثَاء) A soft, plain land

Mālā (مَالَا) Rosary, garland, necklace

Malāhah (مَلَاحَه) Goodly, beautiful and bright

Malīhah (مَلِيحَه) Goodly, bright and beautiful

Manī'ah (مَنِيئَه) A hide in the first stage of tanning

Manīhah (مَنِيحَه) A gift, favor, prize

Mānihah (مَانِحَه) Giver, granter (a gift)

Mannānah (مَنَّانَه) Liberal hearted, generous

Manzah (مَنْزَه) Pious, virtuous, the place at distance

Māridah (مَارِدَه) Lofty, high, sprightliness

Marīnā (مَرِينَا) Elasticity, flexibility, a soft cotton garment

Marīnah (مَرِيْنَه) Elasticity, a soft cotton garment, flexibility

Marjānah (مَرْجَانَه) Coral, small pearls, red beads

Mash'al (مَشْعَل) Lamp, torch, a sort of support for light

Māsitah (مَاسِطَه) A female comber, dresser of hair

Matānah (مَتَانَه) Firmness, solidity

Mathīlah (مَثِيله) Resembling, similar to, illustrious

Ma'ūnah (مُؤُونَه) Provision, store of edibles

Ma'ūnah (مَعُونَه) Aid, help, assistance

Māwarā (مَاوَرَا) Handsome, beautiful

Māzah (مَازَه) Distinguished, separated

Māzijah (مَازِجَه) Mixed, mingled, blended

Mīdhah (مِدْحَه) Praise, eulogy, commendation

Madrah (مَدْره) A noble chief

Midshā (مِدْشا) Lank and slender, one who eats a little

Mihr (مِهْر) Moon, sun, love, attraction

Mihr Jabīn (مِهْر جَبِين) Handsome, having a forehead like the sun

Mihr-un-Nisā' (مِهْرُ النِّسَاء) The most beautiful

Mīrah (مِيرَه) Corn, food, victuals, a soft garment

Mirwā (مِرْوٰى) A thick strong rope

Ma'idah (مَائِدَه) Soft and even land

Mūnā (مُونَا) Pitcher, basket, a big bowl

Muhairah (مُهَيْرَه) A free woman, one whose dowry is dear

Muhsinah (مُحْصِنَه) Chaste, pure, abstaining from indecency

Mu'īzah (مُعيزَه) Indigent, scarcity

Munazzah (مُنَزَّه) Pretty chaste, pure, free

Murūnah (مُرُونَه) Flexibility, pliancy, suppleness

Musarrat (مُسَرَّت) Joy, delight, pleasure

Mutayyibah (مُطَيِّبَه) Perfumed, rendered fragrant

Nabāhat (نَبَاهَت) Insight, intelligence, brightness, spelndor

Nābighah (نَابِغَه) Genius, distinguished

Nabīhah (نَبِيهَه) Distinguished, noble, excellent

Nābijah (نابِجَه) A kind of food of the Arabs

Nabīlah (نَبِيلَه) Noble, highborn, generous, endowed with superior qualities

Nabīqah (نَبِيقَه) Kiot in the branch of grapes

Nābitah (نَابِتَه) Sprouting germinating

Nabītah (نَبِيتَه) The ridges that are raised along edge of rivulets

Nābiyah (نَابِيَه) An elevated or raised place

Nabkhā (نَبْخَا) An elevated and good fertile land

Nabrah (نَبْرَه) Anything rising, emphasis in speaking

Nabtā (نَبْطَا) First water of a

well

Nadā (نَدٰى) Moisture, evening dew, generosity, perfume, liberality

Nidh'ah (نِذعه) Raindrop, softness, slowness

Nādihah (نَادِحَه) To contend for superiority or abundance

Nadīhah (نَدِيحَه) A spacious, wide, roomy, and vast tract

Nādirah (نَادِرَه) Costly, extraordinary, rare

Nādisah (نَادِسَه) Intelligent, sagacious, swift

Nadrah (نَضْرَه) Beauty, brightness, fresh

Nadshā (نَدْشَا) To debate or discuss

Nafīhah (نَفِيحَه) A bow, branch of the tree

Nāfihah (نَافِحَه) A bag of musk

Nafījah (نَفِيجَه) A daughter, cloud, the commencement of anything

Nafīsah (نَفِيسَه) Excellent, valuable, highly prized

Nifkhā (نِفْخَا) An elevated good fertile land

Naghdah (نَغْضَه) A tree, an ostrich

Naghmānah (نَغْمَانَه) Song in a low voice, a tune, totter

Nahdā (نَهْدَا) Soft, tumid land

Nahdah (نَهْدَه) Full, overflowing

Nāhīd (نَاهِيد) The planet Venus

Nahīdah (نَهِيْدَه) Fresh butter, cooked hearts of the grains

Nāhīdah (نَاهِيدَه) The planet, Venus, white and brilliant

Nahīrah (نَهِيرَه) Abundant

Nā'irah (نَائِرَه) Bright, beautiful, attractive

Naihānā (نَيْحَانَا) To move (a branch)

Nailah (نَيْلَه) Something obtained, gained

Na'īmah (نَعِيمَه) Soft, delicate,

fine

Nā'iqah (نَاعِقَه) The caller, preacher, representative

Nā'isah (نَاعِصَه) Helper, assistant

Najāhah (نَجَاحَه) Patience

Najdah (نَجْدَه) Brave, excellent

Najībah (نَجِيبَه) The most excellent, noble, generous

Nājihah (نَاجِحَه) Successful, thriving, prosperous

Najīhah (نَجِيحَه) Successful, patient

Najīzah (نَجِيزَه) Recompense, ready

Namīrah (نَمِيرَه) Sweet and wholesome water

Nāmisah (نَامِسَه) One who indulges in discourse secretly

Nāmiyah (نَامِيَه) Growing, increasing

Namsā' (نَمْسَاء) An Intimate friend

Namshā' (نَمْشَاء) Specked with white and black, decorated

Narjis (نَرْجِس) Narcissus (plant)

Narmīn (نَرْمِين) Delicate, tender, pure and clean

Nashā'ah (نَشَاءَه) A creation, an original production

Nashī'ah (نَشِيئَه) The stone placed on the bottom of a tank, fresh and green plant

Nāshi'ah (نَاشِئَه) Rising in the night, the first hours of the night

Nashibah (نَاشِبَه) One who shoots arrows or maker of arrows

Nāshidah (نَاشِدَه) A woman who gives information, seeks after a stray beast

Nashīdah (نَشِيدَه) To raise voice, chanting, hymn

Nashshābah (نَشَّابَه) One who shoots arrows, maker of

arrows

Nāsibah (نَاسِبَه) An elegant amatory mentioning of a woman in the beginning of a poem

Nāsijah (نَاسِجَه) Weaver

Nasījah (نَسِيجَه) Any woven material

Nasīkah (نَسِيكَه) Sacrifice, a melted piece of gold or silver

Natāshah (نَتَاشَه) Gift of God

Nathīlah (نَثِيلَه) The earth around a wall

Nāthirah (نَاثِرَه) One who disperses, scatters things

Naushābah (نَوْشَابَه) Water of immortality, prominence

Naushīn (نَوْشِيْن) Honey like, sweet

Navīlah (نَوِيلَه) Gift, present

Nawāz (نَوَاز) Favoring, cherishing, kindness

Nāyāb (نَايَاب) Rare, costly, extraordinary

Nayyar (نَيِّر) Luminary, moon, brilliant star

Nayyarā (نَيِّرَا) Luminous, radiant

Nayyarah (نَيِّرَه) Luminous, radiant

Nāz (نَاز) Pride, conceited

Nāzihah (نَازِحَه) A distant or remote dwelling

Nazīhah (نَزِيحَه) One who abstains from indecency, purity of soul

Nāzimah (نَاظِمَه) Organizer, adjuster, one who puts in order

Nāzirah (نَاظِره) The eye, matron, principal, headmistress

Nāzish (نَازِش) Pride, conceit

Nāziyah (نَازِيَه) Proud (of), conceited, agile

Nāzlī (نَازْلِی) Delicacy, softness

Nāznīn (نَازْنِين) Delicate, lovely, sweetheart

Nibtah (نِبْتَه) The manner, form, state

Nidā' (نِداء) To call, sit together in an assembly

Nidāfah (نِدافَه) Trade of carding

Nijdah (نِجْده) Experienced in wars, trial

Nikhat (نِكْهَت) Smell, flavor, relish, savor

Nīlūfar (نِيلُوفَر) A kind of sweet smelling plant, water lily

Nimrah (نِمْرَه) A spot of any color

Nīnūfar (نِينُوفَر) Nenuphar (the great water lily), lotus

Nīqah (نِيقَه) Daintiness, elegance

Nisrīn (نِسْرِين) Jonquil, musk rose

Nitāfah (نِطَافَه) To flow softly, pour out gently

Niyāfah (نِيَافَه) Eminence, (title of honor)

Nudairah (نُدَيْرَه) Rareness, extraordinariness

Nudrat (نُدْرَت) Rarity, main body, extraordinary

Nuhzah (نُهْزَه) An opportunity

Nūnah (نُونَه) A dimple in the chin of a young child

Nusyah (نُسْيَه) Relationship, lineage, parentage

Nushbah (نُشْبَه) Attached, stick to, adhere to

Nuzhat (نُزْهَت) Purity of the soul, pleasure trip, stroll, picnic

Pākīzah (پاكِيْزَه) Clean, tidy, neat

Pārah (پَارَه) Mercury, quick silver, piece

Parwīn (پَرْوِين) Pleiad, a brilliant group

Pashmīnah (پَشْمِينَه) A kind of costly woolen cloth

Qabīnah (قَبِينَه) The sun, sunshine

Qābisah (قَابِصَه) Bodies of

men

Qābiyah (قَابِيَه) A saffron collector

Qā'ibah (قَائِبَه) An egg, young bird

Qandah (قَنْدَه) The honey or juicy like the sugar cane

Qanīt (قَنِيت) A woman who eats a little

Qarīnah (قَرِينَه) Friend, mate, spouse, soul

Qasārah (قَصَارَه) To be short

Qasfah (قَصْفَه) Step of a ladder

Qashībah (قَشِيبَه) White, clean, polished, new, rusty

Qatīn (قَتِين) A skin that retains water, a handsome woman

Qabīsah (قَبِيصَه) A large mass of clay, sand pebbles

Qibānah (قِبَانَه) Job of a weigher

Qibtiyyah (قِبْطِيَّه) A Coptic, copt

Qīndīl (قِنْدِيل) Candle stick, lamp, chandelier

Qisārah (قِصَارَه) To clean, wash, purify

Qubsah (قُبْصَه) Pinch, handful, what one takes in fingers

Qubūnah (قُبُونَه) Act of weighing with the steel yard

Qunābah (قُنَابَه) Combined leaves

Rā'ihah (رَائِحَه) Odor, scent, smell

Rā'iqah (رَائِقَه) A beautiful, comely, attractive woman

Rabāb (رَبَاب) White clouds, a musical instrument

Rabī'ah (رَبِيعَه) A meadow, garden, a stone, a helmet of iron

Rabī'ah (رَبِيئَه) A scout station upon a hill

Rabībah (رَبِيبَه) A step-daughter

Rābidah (رَابِضَه) A certain angel

Rabīdah (رَبِيدَه) A kind of repository

Rābighah (رَابِغَه) Easy, comfortable, having plenty, profitable

Rabīkah (رَبِيكَه) Mire, dates mixed with milk, curd and butter

Rabīlah (رَبِيلَه) Plentifulness, softness, ease and ampleness

Rabīthah (رَبِيثَه) A thing that restrains

Rādibah (رَاضِبَه) Extensive rain, a species of lote tree, moderate

Rādifah (رَادِفَه) A shoot of the palm tree, streaks of fatness

Rādihah (رَادِحَه) Compact, great, heavily laden, plentiful

Rādikhah (رَاضِخَه) To compete in shooting of arrows

Radīkhah (رضيخه) A moderate gift

Radīmah (رَدِيمَه) Garment, pieces of cloth

Rafī'ah (رفيعه) Elevated, high

Rāfighah (رَافِغَه) A benefit, favor, lion

Rāfilah (رَافِلَه) An elegant and beautiful gait, a woman who drags her skirt

Rahāmah (رَحَامَه) Being connected with relationship

Rāhat (رَاحَت) Rest, comfort, tranquility

Rahīdah (رَهِيدَه) Delicate, tender, soft

Rā'i'ah (رَائِعَه) Wonderful, splendid, superb, charming

Raibā (رَيْبَا) Charming, captivating, alluring

Rā'ibah (رَائِبَه) Languid in spirit, confounded

Rā'idah (رَائِدَه) A goodly, soft, tender girl

Raidānah (رَيْدَانَه) Gently blowing wind

Rā'ihah (رَائِحَه) Anything going or returning, a wide

place

Ra'īlah (رَعِيلَه) Advanced party, leading group or generation

Rā'ilah (رَائِلَه) Glutton

Rā'imah (رَائِمَه) A she-camel that loves her offspring

Rā'inah (رَاعِنَه) Foolish, unsound in intellect

Raitah (رَيْطَه) Any covering , a piece of soft and thin cloth

Raithah (رَيْثَه) Slowness, tardiness

Rakhshandah (رَخْشَنْدَه) Bright, resplendent

Ramīdah (رَمِيضَه) Sharpened, made thin

Rāmikah (رَامِكَه) Remaining, staying, abiding in a place

Rāmilah (رَامِلَه) Remaining, staying, one who has little love or affection

Ramīlah (رَمِيلَه) To adorn, weave

Rāmiqah (رَامِقَه) To look long at someone

Rāmisah (رَامِصَه) The wind that rains the dust

Ramīthah (رَمِيْثَه) One who repairs, corrects things

Ramiyyah (رَمِيَّه) An animal of the chase, a game

Ramīzah (رَمِيزَه) Intelligent, prudent, of noble race, agile

Ramlah (رَمْلَه) A little mound of sand

Ramsā' (رَمْصَاء) One of the two little stars

Ramshā' (رَمْشَا) Bouquet, nosegay

Ra'nā (رَعْنَا) A sort of grapes

Rānimah (رَانِمَه) A woman of excellent voice

Ranqah (رَنْقَه) A small quantity of turbid water

Raqīqah (رَقِيقَه) Soft, tender, sensitive

Rāqiyah (رَاقِيَه) A female charmer

Rashā' (رَشَاء) A young gazelle

Rāshāqah (رَشاقَه) Having elegant figure, fine, elegant, chaste

Rāshiqah (رَاشِقَه) To vie with someone in running

Rashīqah (رَشِيقَه) A goodly, beautiful and slender girl

Rāsilah (رَاسِلَه) To send a letter

Rāsimah (رَاسِمَه) A she-camel that goes at a certain pace

Ra'thah (رَعْثَه) A large pearl

Rathī'ah (رَثِيئَه) A mixture of sour and fresh milk

Rātinah (رَاطِنَه) Slow pace, a thread

Rauhīn (رَوْهِين) Hard, strong, iron

Raumīnah (رَوْمِينَه) A loving lady

Razānah (رَزَانَه) Gravity, dignity of manner, good performance

Razīnah (رَزِينَه) Firm, constant and grave, modest

Rī'ah (رِيعَه) A high mound, hill, elevated place

Ribā'ah (رِبَاعَه) Obligation, responsibility

Ribābah (رِبَابَه) Tenths, a covenant, confederacy

Rībālah (رِيبَالَه) Crafty, intelligent, lion

Ribdah (رِبْدَه) Sharpened, to make thin

Ribdhah (رِبْذَه) The wisp, piece of wool

Ridā' (رِدَاء) Robe, gown, suit of any kind

Rīdah (رِيْدَه) Gently blowing wind

Rīmā (رِيمَا) White antelope, gazelle,a female gazelle

Rimāmah (رِمَامَه) The art of making lances

Rimthah (رِمْثَه) To arrange, mend, wipe with the hand

Rinā (رِينَا) A princess

Ritānah (رِطَانَه) To use a language not generally understood

Rithdah (رِثْدَه) A company, a numerous staying company

Rizān (رِزَان) Elevated, hard ground with water

Rūbah (رُوبَه) Ferment

Rubdah (رُبْضَه) Remaining stationary, a manner of lying upon breast

Rubdah (رُبْدَه) A dust color, a color inclining to blackness

Rubsah (رُبْصَه) An expecting, waiting, tarrying in expectation

Rubyah (رُبْيَه) A species of small animal, a moderate, small gift

Rudākhah (رُضَاخَه) A moderate gift

Rūfiyah (رُوْفِيَه) Merciful, compassionate

Rughābah (رُغَابَه) The smallest, minor

Rukānah (رُكَانَه) Firmness, solidity, gravity

Rukhsānah (رُخْسَانَه) Handsome, beautiful

Rukhsārah (رُخْسَارَه) Face, countenance

Rumthah (رُمثَه) Fresh milk, excellent quality

Rūmīlah (رُوْمِيلَه) A female weaver, one who adorns

Rumaisā' (رُمَيْصَاء) One of the two little stars

Rumāmah (رُمَامَه) Sufficiency of the means of substance, thriving state

Rūmānah (رُومَانَه) A steel yard, a knob of metal or wood

Rumdah (رُمْدَه) Dust color

Rumkah (رُمْكَه) Dusky, dingy, a certain color of camels

Ruqaiqah (رُقَيْقَه) Thin, soft, sensitive

Rūshān (رُوْشَان) Bright, shining stars

Sabā (صَبَا) The east wind

Sabahah (صَبَاحَه) Beauty, comeliness, elegance

Sabhā (صَبْحَا) A female clear and fair in the forehead

Sabīkah (سَبِيكَه) Ingot, bar of gold or silver

Sābilah (سَابِلَه) A much traveled road

Sabīn (سَبِين) A woman having black garment for the lower part

Sabītā (سَبِيتَا) Vest, leisure

Subāb (صُبَاب) A portion or small quantity

Sabiyyah (صَبِيَّه) A girl, young woman

Sabrah (سَبْرَه) A cold morning, morning after sunrise

Sabrīnā (سَبْرِينَا) The princess

Sabtah (سَبْطَه) Tall, lank, of good stature, easy

Sabūhī (صَبُوْحِي) Morning draught of liquor

Sadaf (صَدَف) Oyster shell, anything high

Sa'dah (صَعْدَه) A high, elevated piece of land

Sadānah (سَدَانَه) Minister or servant of the Ka'bah

Sādiyah (سَادِيَه) A woman of high quality

Saf'ā' (سَفْعَاء) Black inclining to redness, a constant blowing wind

Sāfinah (سَافِنَه) A wind that blows gently

Saffānah (سَفَّانَه) A pearl

Sāfi'ah (سَافِعَه) A woman who is bold to attack, assault

Sāfiqah (صَافِقَه) A company of men

Safīrah (صَفِيرَه) A dam between two tracts of land

Safītah (سَفِيطَه) Cheerful, happy, beautiful, liberal

Safiyyah (صَفِيَّه) Pure, unmixed, chosen, sincere friend

Sāfiyyah (صَافِيَّه) Things belonging to Allāh, villages and towns

Safūrā (صَفُورَا) To be empty, exalted, wife of Mūsā ﷺ

Safwā' (سَفْوَاء) A swift wind

Safwā' (صَفْوَاء) A broad and smooth stone

Safwānah (صَفْوَانَه) A hard and smooth stone

Sahbā' (صَهْبَاء) Red wine, red and white mixed

Sahīmah (سَهِيمَه) Partner

Sāhirah (سَاهِرَه)Awake, vigilant, watchful, the moon

Sahmā (سَحْمَا) Black cloud, a certain plant, she-camel

Sahnā' (سَحْنَاء) A form, aspect, appearance

Sahrish (سَحْرِش) Bewitching like a morning, charming

Sā'ibah (صَائِبَه) Right, correct, hitting the mark

Sā'idah (سَاعِدَه) Helper, assistant, supporting beam

Sā'imah (سَائِمَه) Grazing animals

Sa'īrah (سَعِيرَه) A sign, mark

Sajāfah (سَجَافَه) A pair of curtains

Sajāhah (سَجَاحَه) Gentleness, easiness

Sajal (سَجَل) Full bucket, gift, scroll, public document

Sajhā' (سَجْحَاء) A beautiful she-camel

Sāji'ah (سَاجِعَه) Pursuing a right course or direction, shining

Saji'ah (سَجِيعَه) A woman of fine disposition

Sajīhah (سَجِيحَه) A gentle, easy disposition

Sajil (سَجِل) Fine, well arranged, orderly

Sajīlah (سَجِيلَه) A large bucket

Sakhīnah (سَخِينَه) A kind of food made of mild dates and flour

Salī'ah (سَلِيعَه) Nature, disposition

Salījah (سَلِيجَه) A squared piece of wood

Sālimah (سَالِمَه) To make peace or reconciliation

Samalah (سَمَلَه) A small quantity of water

Samāmah (سَمَامَه) Mountain swallows, a swift she camel

Saman (سَمَن) Jasmine

Sawīlah (سَوِيلَه) Equal, handsome

Samīnah (سَمِينَه) A plump woman, a land of good soil with stones

Samnah (سَمْنَه) A certain herb having white flowers

Samrā' (سَمْرَاء) Brunette, wheat-loaves flour

Sandaisā (سَنْدِيسَا) Message, good news

Sandarah (سَنْدَرَه) To go quickly, hastily, a certain tree

Sanhā' (سَنْهَآء) A palm tree

Sanī'ah (سَنِيْعَه) Well formed, having fine limbs

Sanīlah (سَنِيلَه) Good natured

Sanīmah (سَنِيمَه) Raised, elevated, high

Sāniyah (سَانِيَه) A she-camel for drawing water

Sanūbar (صَنُوبَر) Pine, any cane bearing tree

Sārā (سَارَا) Pure, excellent, sweet-smelling

Sārah (سَارَه) The princess, name of the wife of Ibrāhīm عليه السلام

Sarhah (سَرْحَه) A beautiful plant growing on water, exterior yard of a house

Sāribah (سَارِبَه) Pole, column, staff

Sarībah (سَرِيبَه) A sheep or goat turned from water

Sārihah (سَارِحَه) A certain kind of tree

Sarītā (سَرِيتَا) Clever, active, intelligent

Sarūj (سَرُوج) Lotus, flower

Sarūsh (سَرُوش) Angel,

voice from heaven, voice of prophecy

Satwat (سَطْوَت) Attack, assault, a disposition

Saubiyah (صَوبِيَه) Right in opinion

Saulat (صَوْلَت) Impetuosity, violence, force, power to rule

Sha'bā' (شَعْبَاء) A gazelle, goat, gap between horns

Shabānah (شَبَانَه) Of night

Shabī'ah (شَبِيعَه) Intelligent, strong, satisfied, satiated

Shabnam (شَبْنَم) Dew, fine linen, lawn

Shād (شَاد) Glad, cheerful, delighted

Shādhah (شَاذَه) Anything apart, alone

Shādhiyah (شَاذِيَه) A unique odor, fragrance

Shafaq (شَفَق) Compassion, tender, evening twilight

Shafīqah (شَفِيقَه) Compassionate, tender, fearful, anxious

Shaguftah (شَگُفْتَه) Blooming, cheerful

Shāhānah (شَاهَانَه) Royal, regal, splendid

Shāhīn (شَاهِين) Falcon, Iqbal's symbol for a Muslim youth

Shāhīnah (شَاهِينَه) Small falcon

Shahlā (شَهْلَا) A want, need, tinge, beautiful black eyes

Shahnāz (شَهْنَاز) Bride, a musical tune

Shahzain (شَهْزَيْن) Extremely handsome, beautiful

Shaibā' (شَيْبَآء) Virgin

Shailā (شَيْلَا) Complete

Shā'istah (شَائِسْتَه) Polite, suitable, cultured

Shā'izah (شَائِزَه) Unique, extraordinary

Shajī'ah (شَجِيْعَه) Courageous, bold, brave

Shakībah (شَكِيبَه) Patient, tolerant

Shāradā (شَارَدَا) Native cuckoo

Shama‘ (شَمَع) Candle, lamp

Shamā’ilah (شَمَائِلَه) Character, temper, natural

Shamīlah (شَمِيلَه) Unification, unity

Shamīm (شَمِيم) Fragrance, front breeze

Shāmirah (شامِرَه) An ewe, she goat

Shamīrah (شَمِيرَه) Active, quick out oneself vigorously

Shāmisah (شامِسَه) A noble, chaste lady

Shārzah (شَارْزَه) A bird

Shārībah (شَارِبَه) A party living on the bank of a river

Sharidah (شَرِيدَه) Driven away, expelled

Shāridah (شَارِدَه) A fleeing lioness, she camel

Shārifah (شَارِفَه) High and advanced in age

Sharmīn (شَرْمِين) Modest, delicate

Shāziyah (شَازِيَه) High, exalted, elevated

Shibrah (شِبْرَه) Gift, wealth, faculties

Shīmā (شِيمَا) Halite, nature, fragrance

Shīmah (شِيمَه) Small, habit, nature, fragrance

Shimlah (شِمْلَه) Cloak

Shīrīn (شِيرِين) Sweet, mellow

Shīzā (شِيزٰى) A kind of black wood

Shu‘airā (شُعَيْرَا) A kind of trees, noble

Shumailah (شُمَيْلَه) Good natured, noble

Shumaisah (شُمَيْسَه) A tall and straight tree

Sibyah (صَبِيَه) A young woman, girl

Sīdānah (سِيدَانَه) A woman of high rank, quality

Sidānah (سِدَانَه) Minister, servant at the Ka'bah

Sifānah (سِفَانَه) The craft of constructing ships, boats

Silkānah (سِلْكَانَه) The young one of the partridge

Sīmah (سِيمَه) Handsome

Sīmī (سِيْمِي) Silvery

Sīmīn (سِيمِين) Silvery, brilliant, beautiful

Sināhah (سِنَاحَه) The veil, covering

Sināyah (سِنَايَه) Anything complete, whole

Sarwah (سَرْوَه) An arrow broad in the head

Soniyā (سَوْنِيَا) Wisdom, intelligence, a goldsmith

Soudānah (سَوْدَانَه) A certain bird that eats grapes

Sumaikah (سُمَيْكَه) A little fish

Sūbiyah (سُوبِيَه) A kind of beverage prepared from wheat

Su'dā (سُعْدٰي) Forunate, happy, prosperous

Suffāhah (صُفَّاحَه) Anything broad and wide

Sūfiyah (صُوْفِيَه) Mystic, pious

Suhaibah (سُحَيْبَه) Remains of water in a pool, a covering

Suhairah (سُهَيْرَه) One who keeps awake at night

Sumā (سُمَا) A star

Sumaikā (سُمَيْكَا) A certain small dried fish

Sumānā (سُمَانٰى) A quail

Sumlah (سُمْلَه) A small quantity of water

Sumnah (سُمْنَه) A certain herb having white flowers

Sumrah (سُمْرَه) Brownness, tanny

Sumtah (صُمْتَه) Silence, muteness, speechless

Sunaihah (سُنَيْهَه) A year

Sunayyah (سُنَيَّه) A year, a single revolution of the sun

Sunbul (سُنْبُل) Ear of corn, spurned

Sundar (سُنْدَر) A beautiful, pretty woman

Suraitā' (سُرَيْطَاء) A kind of food

Surwah (سُرْوَه) An arrow broad in the head

Tābān (تَابَان) Glittering, splendid

Tabānah (تَبَانَه) The place, house, sagacious, prudent

Tābindah (تَابِنْدَه) Bright, luminous

Tahmīnah (تَهْمِينَه) Suspicious, who blames others

Tājwar (تَاجْوَر) Sovereign

Talbīnah (تَلْبِينَه) A certain food made of flour, milk and honey

Talī'ah (طَلِيعَه) A scout

Tāli'ah (طَالِعَه) Rising, appearing

Talīqah (طَلِيقَه) Cheerful, freed, emancipated

Tamādir (تَمَاضِر) Fat and healthy

Tāniyā (تَانِيَا) Fairy, peri

Tāniyah (تَانِيَه) Voice of a deer

Tāriqah (طَارِقَه) Event that occurs in the night

Tarīrah (طَرِيرَه) Handsome, a young woman

Tasbīh (تَسْبِيح) A fleshy man

Tāshifah (تَاشِفَه) Kind, affectionate

Tazmīn (تَزْمِين) Possessing good qualities

Thabīn (ثَبِين) The extremity of one's garment to fold or carry things

Thabyā (ثَبْيَا) To collect, enlarge, add

Tha'dah (ثَعْدَه) Soft, tender, fresh, juicy

Thamīlah (ثَمِيلَه) Remains of food, herbage, rock

Thamrā (ثَمْرَا) Abounding with fruit

Thanā (ثَنَا) Praise, eulogy, commendation

Thāniyah (ثَانِيَه) A second, a moment

Thaniyyah (ثَنِيَّه) A road in or upon a moutain, front teeth

Thaqībah (ثَقِيبَه) Having much milk

Thariyyah (ثَرِيَّه) Moist, humidity

Tharwah (ثَرْوَه) Abundance, possessing much property

Tharwat (ثَرْوَت) Plenty, wealth, riches

Tharyā (ثَرْيَا) Moister soft land

Thu'ālah (ثُعَالَه) Certain herbage or a plant

Thumālah (ثُمَالَه) A remainder, a little water remaining

Thumlah (ثُمْلَه) Grain and meat of parched barley

Thunā' (ثُنَاء) By twos, two and two

Thurayyā (ثُرَيَّا) The pleiad, chandelier, cluster of lamps

Thuwaibah (ثُوَيْبَه) To return, foster mother of the Prophet ﷺ

Tībah (طِيبَه) The well of Zamzam, pleasant, lawful

Tūbā (طُوبٰى) A pleasant life

'Ufrah (عُفْرَه) The feathers around the neck of a cock, the dust

Ujālā (اُجَالَا) Light, sunshine, to be lighted

Umm Rūmān (اُمِّ رُوْمَان) Fiction, love story (mother of 'Āishah ﷺ)

Unūsh (اُنُوش) Cheerful, glad

'Urainah (عُرَيْنَه) Lair, den

'Urbānah (عُرْبَانَه) A pure and earnest money, carriage

Urfah (اُرْفَه) A limit, boundary, to make a separation

'Uwainah (عُوَيْنَه) Protection

Wābidah (وَابِضَه) Clever,

swift, intelligent

Wabīsah (وَبيصَه) A live coal, bright

Wābisah (وَابصَه) Shining, gleaning, glistening

Wadī'ah (وَضيئَه) Beautiful, fair, neat and clean

Wadī'ah (وَديعَه) Trust, consignment, deposit

Wadīmah (وَضيمَه) A morning entertainment

Wāsilah (وَاسِلَه) Means, favor, honor

Wajī'ah (وَجيئَه) Dates moistened with milk, and butter

Wadā'ah (وَدَاعَه) Gentleness, mildness

Wardah (وَرْدَه) Rose, red flower, evening at the time of sunset

Wāriqah (وَارِقَه) Verdant, green

Warqah (وَرْقَه) Leaf, sheet, folio, record

Wasāmah (وَسَامَه) Traits of beauty

Washāhah (وَشَاحَه) Saber, sword

Wāshijah (وَاشِجَه) Attached in the manner of a net, intricate

Washījah (وَشِيجَه) The root of a tree

Wāshirah (وَاشِرَه) A woman who sharpens her teeth

Washmah (وَشْمَه) Early sprouting of grass, plan, first drop of rain

Washayā (وَشَيَا) A date having a thick bark

Wāsimah (وَاسِمَه) Handsome, good-looking, comely

Wasīmah (وَسِيمَه) Traits of beauty, handsome

Wasīqah (وَسِيقَه) A mob, troop of camels

Wasīrah (وَصِيرَه) Written statement of bargain

Wathījah (وَثِيجَه) Land of thick, dense, herbage

Wāthilah (وَاثِلَه) A hard rope

Wurdah (وُرْدَه) A bright, bay color

Yāfi'ah (يافعه) High mountain, a difficult matter, young woman

Yāsirah (يَاسِرَه) Gentle, fragile

Yasmīn (يَاسْمِين) Jasmine

Zā'irah (زائره) A visitor, guest

Zabānah (زَبَانَه) A flame, brilliant light, glow

Zabībah (زبيبَه) Raisins, dried figs

Zābinah (زَابِنَه) An elevated place to push, to thrust vehemently

Zabyah (ظَبْيَه) A young woman, a certain animal

Zafīfah (زَفِيفَه) Light and quick

Zāfirah (زَافِرَه) One who carries load, Chieftess, mistress

Zaib (زِيب) Ornament, beauty, elegance

Za'īmah (زَعِيمَه) Chief, leader, spokeswoman, strong

Zain (زَين) Good, beautiful, a kind of tree

Zainab (زَيْنَب) A beautiful and sweet small tree

Za'īnah (ظَعِينَه) Woman's litter, woman in a litter

Zalījah (زَلِيجَه) Quick and swift she-camel

Zaman (زَمَن) A time

Zamurrad (زَمُرَّد) The emerald

Zārā (زَارَا) Crop of bird, a group

Zārah (زَارَه) Crop of a bird

Zarash (زَرَش) Costly, wealthy

Zar Fashān (زَرْفَشَان) Charitable, bountiful, lustrous

Zarībah (زَرِيبَه) A hunter, shooter, archer

Zarīn (زَرِين) Gold, golden

Zarīnah (زَرِينَه) Golden or gold things, made of gold

Zārīnah (زَارينه) Queen of Russia (title)

Zarīrah (زَرِيره) Intelligent, sagacious, quick

Zarmīnah (زَرْمِينَه) A wealthy woman

Zarrīn (زَرِّين) Bright, glittering

Zawbiyah (زَوْبِيَه) The gift of God

Zaufā (زوْفَا) Hyssop (plant)

Zībā (زِيبَا) Adorned, beautiful, graceful, proper

Zinnīrah (زِنّيره) The small pebbles

Zufrah (زُفْرَه) Drawing back breath vehemently

Zuhairah (زُهَيْرَه) Shining, bright, beautiful

Zuhrah (زُهْرَه) Splendour, beauty, the planet Venus

Zulaikhā (زُلَيْخَا) A handsome woman

Zunnārah (زُنَّارَه) The small pebbles